# DESIGN LITERACIES

*Design Literacies: Learning and Innovation in the Digital Age* explores new ways of meaning-making by examining the practices, stories, and products of new and digital media producers with the goal of understanding the logic of marketplace production.

Based on interviews with 32 new media and digital technology producers, including designers of video games, community activists, and marketers of digital technologies, *Design Literacies* looks at the shared patterns and common themes and offers a window into contemporary out-of-school practices, a language to describe these practices, and a pedagogy that better meets students' needs in this new media and digital age.

With a foreword by Gunther Kress and an afterword by James Paul Gee, both key figures in this field, *Design Literacies: Learning and Innovation in the Digital Age* will be of interest to students of applied linguistics, composition and rhetoric, media studies, and education.

**Mary P. Sheridan** is Associate Professor of English and Director of Composition at the University of Wyoming, USA. Her previous publications include *Girls, Feminism, and Grassroots Literacies: Activism in the GirlZone* (2008) and *Feminism and Composition: A Critical Sourcebook* (co-edited with Gesa Kirsch, Lance Massey, Lee Nickoson-Massey, and Faye Spencer Maor, 2003).

**Jennifer Rowsell** is Assistant Professor of Literacy Education and Coordinator of the English Education Program at Rutgers Graduate School of Education, New Brunswick, New Jersey, USA. Her previous publications include *Literacy and Education: Understanding New Literacy Studies in the Classroom* (co-written with Kate Pahl, 2005), *Travel Notes from the New Literacy Studies* (co-written with Kate Pahl, 2006), and *Family Literacy Experiences* (2006).

# LITERACIES
## Series Editor: David Barton
### *Lancaster University*

Literacy practices are changing rapidly in contemporary society in response to broad social, economic and technological changes: in education, the workplace, the media and in everyday life. This series reflects the burgeoning research and scholarship in the field of literacy studies and its increasingly interdisciplinary nature. The series aims to provide a home for books on reading and writing which consider literacy as a social practice and which situate it within broader institutional contexts. The books develop and draw together work in the field; they aim to be accessible, interdisciplinary and international in scope, and to cover a wide range of social and institutional contexts.

**LITERACY, LIVES AND LEARNING**
*David Barton, Roz Ivanič, Yvon Appleby, Rachel Hodge and Karin Tusting*

**LITERACY, GENDER AND ATTAINMENT**
*Gemma Moss*

**HIPHOP LITERACIES**
*Elaine Richardson*

**LITERACY IN THE NEW MEDIA AGE**
*Gunther Kress*

**CITY LITERACIES**
Learning to Read across Generations and Cultures
*Eve Gregory and Ann Williams*

**LITERACY AND DEVELOPMENT**
Ethnographic Perspectives
*Edited by Brian V. Street*

**SITUATED LITERACIES**
Theorising Reading and Writing in Context
*Edited by David Barton, Mary Hamilton and Roz Ivanič*

**MULTILITERACIES**
Literacy Learning and the Design of Social Futures
*Edited by Bill Cope and Mary Kalantzis*

**GLOBAL LITERACIES AND THE WORLD-WIDE WEB**
*Edited by Gail E. Hawisher and Cynthia L. Selfe*

**STUDENT WRITING**
Access, Regulation, Desire
*Theresa M. Lillis*

**SILICON LITERACIES**
Communication, Innovation and Education in the Electronic Age
*Edited by Ilana Snyder*

**AFRICAN AMERICAN LITERACIES**
*Elaine Richardson*

**GRASSROOTS LITERACIES**
*Jan Blommaert*

# DESIGN LITERACIES

## Learning and Innovation in the Digital Age

*Mary P. Sheridan and Jennifer Rowsell*

LONDON AND NEW YORK

First edition published 2010 by Routledge
2 Park Square, Milton Park, Abingdon OX14 4RN

Simultaneously published in the USA and Canada by Routledge
270 Madison Ave, New York, NY 10016

*Routledge is an imprint of the Taylor & Francis Group, an informa business*

© 2010 Mary P. Sheridan and Jennifer Rowsell

Typeset in Baskerville by The Running Head, Cambridge,
www.therunninghead.com
Printed and bound in Great Britain by CPI Antony Rowe, Chippenham, Wiltshire

*British Library Cataloguing in Publication Data*
A catalogue record for this book is available from the British Library

*Library of Congress Cataloging in Publication Data*
A catalog record for this book has been requested

ISBN 10: 0–415–55962–6 (hbk)
ISBN 10: 0–415–55964–5 (pbk)

ISBN13: 978–0–415–55962–1 (hb)
ISBN13: 978–0–415–55964–2 (pb)

# CONTENTS

# FIGURES AND TABLES

## Figures

## Tables

# ACKNOWLEDGMENTS

We would like to thank our interviewee participants for generously sharing their expertise and thoughts on design. We owe our gratitude to Gunther Kress and James Paul Gee for their thoughtful responses to our book and for their work that set us on course for our research.

Editing is a silent, strong force in a manuscript and two individuals who contributed to the voice and clarity of the book are Tara McGowan and in particular the consummate editor of clarity and precision, Caroline Cole. Without Caroline's guidance and feedback throughout the writing process, it would have been a challenge to say what we wanted to say. We would like to express our gratitude for the stewardship of Sophie Jacques at Routledge and the deft and detailed editorial work of Kit Scorah.

Mary P. would like to thank Mary Pauline, Luke, and Aidan, whose joy is contagious. Jennifer would like to thank Fred, Maddie, and Kierra for enduring hours of her hunched over a computer.

# FOREWORD

*Gunther Kress, Professor of Semiotics and Education,*
*Institute of Education, University of London*

"Be fearlessly creative!" "Be fearless innovators!" the authors enjoin their read-ers, and they themselves practice what they preach. They take us into the world where people *do* things, *make* texts, games, sites for participation, in the unforgiv-ing environment of "the market." We are given a good look at this world and the circumstances in which meanings are produced. The people to whom we are introduced have worked in many ways in different parts of the "meaning industries"; they have made choices based on dissatisfactions as much as on ideals and values about the world in which they act and which they want to become different.

Having jumped, feet first, into a world so differently paced to that of the school and so differently constituted, the authors need terms to describe it for themselves and for us, describe what it is about and give us a sense of those who are actors in it. As with the European "explorers" of yore, they have brought labels with them, though these don't really seem to fit too well to name these exotic things. Fearless as their precept, the authors record not just the actions, the processes, but also the "language" of the locals: instead of "dis-course," "genre," "voice," "style," they have "spin"; our "audience" seems to be their "architectures of participation"; and "reading" and "communication" are "meaningful traffic" in a "digital space"—not pages, nor even a screen. The rhetorical task of making messages apt for an audience is motivated by anxieties about being "filtered out" in the noise of the market of messages; and "the case studies illustrate how producers forge dispositions focused on hitting the audi-ence with the right message through the right text."

This *is* a different world.

What we see here is definitely not the world of the official literacy curricula of anglo-phone societies; what we *are* shown is the world of semiotic production, the making of things that mean or which can be used in making meaning. For us, as readers, the real challenge is that of *recognition*—the term the authors have brought in from the work of another fearless explorer—the anthropologist Mar-garet Mead. So, for us, the readers, the task is to retune our vision to *see* what there actually is; to *recognize* what principles are at issue; to *understand* what counts as knowledge here, how it is made, by whom and for whom? How do we find means to *recognize* what counts as learning and how it happens here? The old tools won't help us here: they were made to show up different things in another world. "What entities are used in contemporary compositions?," "What principles of composition are at work here?" are questions asked before, but which have become central here, right now. The new entities are neither "letters" nor "words," though they are likely to occur; nor are the principles of composition much like the syntax that had been fashioned by long histories of semiotic work in which the *temporal* ordering of speech was transducted into the *linearity* of written texts—in cultures with alphabetic scripts at any rate. Composition here happens with *modular* entities, fashioned newly for each occasion, in spatial, *non-linear* arrangements, made for the occasion. Existing cultural resources are treated as quarries for semiotic materials, much as abandoned or half-destroyed castles, palaces, monasteries had been, in Europe and elsewhere, over centuries, by pragmatic locals: "this column here can be a lintel on the new doorway." The authors exhort educators "to move away from over-valuing 'original research' and move towards teaching effective ways to *remix* existing information to help students better meet today's opportunities and problems."

"Remix" is another of these local terms, unlikely to be found in the literacy curriculum of any school-system. If we were to rummage around for a term from the older stock of tools/labels to match it as near as could be, "plagiarism" might come up as the most likely candidate. Yet the implied contrast in the quote above—"original research" versus "remix"—shows up the difficulty of *recognition* for all of us: is "remix"—the semiotic work of younger generations— less "original," less likely to serve as a means for doing "research" than the work their predecessors had done with their means? Having left the staid land of (traditional) "literacy" and wandered into the less well-ordered land of popular culture, it behoves us to try, at least, to uncover, to understand the principles of "remix": what principles of selection are at work, what principles of arrangement, of making the new by using the old to meet contemporary demands. Looked at in that way, some of the strangeness may give way to recognition, for there seems much that is similar, familiar even, to the traditional purposes and processes of what was never, in any case, "original research." Are we, the authors ask, prepared and capable of recognizing these contemporary means as suitable for conducting "original research"?

In fashioning or "forging" the units for composition, the semiotic eye of those who design and shape contemporary compositions are differently focused than the eyes of their predecessors—and teachers: focused on "stuff" that can serve as apt bearers of meaning, focused more on *information* maybe than on form, on information as form and on form as information, ready to be transformed by the bricoleur-designers into knowledge-as-tool, not recognized by their teachers, given the entire novelty of the tasks.

Implied in all this is the second big issue, that of fashioning an apt new idiom: one with terms that will serve better than those with which we struggle to understand the world of "production." The "idiom" here is that of those who *do*, who *make*, who fuss about *getting it right* more than about *naming it right*: or maybe, naming it right in the domain in which they work: "spin," "meaningful traffic," "digital space," anxiety about being "filtered out." It is the idiom both of the "forge" and of the "market" and those who work in either. In this—as in many markets, in many places—you do have to shout, and maybe hitting the customers is just what you do need to do; though "playful design" is shown as another means for not "getting filtered out."

And of course, in the world where the market is dominant, the rules of the market shape habitus, subjectivity, identity. Markets are about choice; and the semiotic work of selecting from the choices available to me is the work of making my identity. *Style* is the result of the sum of choices I have made; *style* defines who I am. *Aesthetics* is the social valuation of *style*, and so there is a struggle for valuation expressed in terms of style and aesthetics. Power is present everywhere: possibilities of choice are governed by power in various forms, and the social evaluation of style is an outcome of social power. Identity is at issue everywhere and absolutely. The aesthetics of the school correspond in no way to the aesthetics of those who have made their own, different choices in the market: the products of choices and valuations made by "authority" for others are not a saleable commodity in this market.

One well-known response by the school is what the authors call the "retro-fitting of content." We are all familiar with the urgency with which this, the Holy Grail of Education, is being pursued: "harnessing" the potentials of the new technologies to the purposes of the school—the major means employed by the school in the struggle to be heard, to be a participant, not to be filtered out. And so, huge amounts of effort and money are given over to "retrofitting" the school's content to technologies—"games" are perhaps the most prominent instance—whose social affordances demand a pedagogy of participation and a curriculum shaped by the requirements of social spaces very differently conceived and differently imagined to those of the school.

The nub of the book's concern remains with the school, but now with the insights brought by "production": *is there, and if there is, what is the continuing role and place for the school?* In the market of idioms there is a struggle for which idiom is to rule. The profoundly different interests, values, principles of selection, of style and of aesthetics, leave the school, as it is constituted at the moment, with neither attractiveness nor legitimacy. Yet there is the question: will the idioms of popular culture, of the market, of individuated choice be sufficient for those who are now turning away from the school in their lives out of school? Or for that still large group with a deeply held and widely shared sense of the importance of common responsibility and sociality?

For me the questions are: "What cultural capital is provided in any one site?" "What cultural resources are offered by any one idiom?" "What cultural capital is offered in each domain and what access does each provide?" and "What is not offered in any one domain and its idiom which might be essential for the health of the community?" The book, while pointing insistently to "production," also acknowledges that domains and idioms concerned with reflection and understanding have not become redundant, by any means. Many of those who are concerned with *doing*, with *making*, with *getting it right*, are concerned with *reflecting* and *theorizing*, even if they might name it differently. There is a division of labor—or maybe, better, there is a distinction in focus of concerns. To flourish, a community must retain its interest in the idioms which foreground reflection and theorization as well as in the domains of doing and making. In the market of idioms it is essential to foster both perspectives so as to provide means of seeing and naming differently, ways that tell us what kinds of spin there are, what "spin" actually is, what its ideological components are, and for whose benefit and in whose service particular forms of spin are produced. In short, we need to foster all the idioms that provide us with essential naming, essential to the social and ethical well-being of all of us.

The task of merging the idioms or to provide useable translations, lies with those whose task it is to reflect and theorize, to provide understanding of what is happening in the world of doing and making. That seems the authors' suggestion as well. But above all they want us to look, eyes open, where they are pointing us.

This is not a timid book. It arrives with a thump and it makes a big noise. Anyone concerned with such issues can't afford not to go and find out what the noise is all about. It aims to make us look differently. It did that for me.

# 1

# THE PROBLEM-SOLVING
# LOGIC OF DIGITAL MEDIA
# PRODUCTION

*The skills to read something on the screen and the skills to read something on paper are fundamentally different* . . . I know I've seen lots of people who are highly educated people who are like painfully slow at reading a web page because they just don't know. They sort of see everything that's there. If you get a printed page in a book you sort of expect to read all of it but on a webpage there's only probably a third of it if you take out navigational artifacts and flying banners and all sorts of things. If you remove all that stuff you're probably down to almost a third of what's on the screen—and people who just read books don't get that. *You know, it's a new way of learning.*

(Paul Taylor, computer programmer/website designer/
inventor, 2007; emphasis added)

Paul Taylor (pseudonym)[1] articulates what national reports, newspaper headlines, and our own felt sense indicate: reading and composing in today's digitally mediated age requires a whole "new way of learning." One reason is the changed context of what it means to communicate effectively today. Exponential growth in knowledge, interconnectedness of opportunities, and globally networked communication technologies both afford and demand new ways to share and create information—a task many primarily text-based readers seem to find difficult.

Such transformations illustrate that we are living in what anthropologist Margaret Mead might call a time of radical cultural change. Writing 40 years ago, Mead (1970) schematized that cultures respond to significant changes in one of three ways: "*postfigurative*, in which children learn primarily from their forebears, *cofigurative*, in which both children and adults learn from their peers, and *prefigurative*, in which adults learn from their children" (1; emphasis in original). For Mead, most cultures were experiencing prefigurative change, largely due to expansive technological changes: "Today, suddenly, because all the peoples of the world are part of one electronically based, intercommunicating network, young people everywhere share a kind of experience that none of the elders ever have had or will have" (50). This trend of becoming electronically interconnected—which continues in the world today—means that youth have been experiencing, and by extension, *designing* cultures that their elders would never have imagined. The effect of this radical shift in technological interconnectedness has meant that

> We must, in fact, teach ourselves how to alter adults' behavior so that we can give up postfigurative upbringing, with its tolerated cofigurative components, and discover prefigurative ways of teaching and learning that will keep the future open. We must create new models for adults who can teach their children not what to learn, but how to learn and not what they should be committed to, but the value of commitment.
>
> (Mead 1970: 72)

As the title of her book *Culture and Commitment* indicates, Mead's investment in understanding large-scale cultural changes calls her not only to understand this change, but also to think through how to help communities adapt, in large part by having elders—those doing the traditional teaching—learn how to participate meaningfully in this altered environment and help youth to do the same.

We share Mead's assessment of the radical role technology plays in shaping today's culture, though our focus is more limited to issues of literacy and learning. And, like Mead, we want to investigate both what is driving this transformation (in our case, the logics of those creating new, digitally mediated environments for literacy and learning) and how we can help elders (in our case, educators) adjust so that they can better prepare youth to handle and shape what their elders never faced. Yet, as Paul notes in the quotation that opens this chapter, merely applying traditional skills to today's context is not effective.

Although many educators acknowledge this fact, academic curricula often lag behind the rapid transformations that reshape what students and teachers need to know to design and participate in today's changing world (UNESCO 2004).[2] Standardized testing (e.g. SAT, the IOWA Test of Basic Skills, GCSE) and uniform national curricula elicit pedagogies built on a Fordist assembly-line model where students specialize in recalling or perhaps recreating existing structures—structures often outdated in a prefigurative world. Instead of this model, we argue that pedagogies need a different production logic, what Mead may call a cofigurative or even prefigurative logic that accounts for a range of innovative meaning-making practices needed to problem solve in contemporary contexts. This logic cannot be retrofitted with well-trodden conceptions of being literate nor taught by elders locked in a traditional, print-only mindset. Furthermore, we argue that this logic, which promotes dispositions that may not have been highly valued in previous generations, should be the basis for contemporary pedagogy.

2

These co- and prefigurative production logics call us to rework traditional pedagogies to be responsive to today's conditions. Such pedagogies build upon basic skills as well as develop broader competencies that enable people to, in the case of literacy pedagogies, meaningfully create and interact with complex practices that locate literacy within "cultural processes, personal circumstances and collective structures" (UNESCO 2004: 6). We posit that these pedagogies should be based on "design literacies," with "design" capturing how producers rework given materials to better suit their needs and opportunities (cf New London Group 2000) and "literacies" capturing "a continuum of learning [that is] enabling individuals to achieve their goals, to develop their knowledge and potential, and to participate fully in their community and wider society" (UNESCO 2004: 13). Such design literacies, we argue, will help people become problem-solvers in today's pre- and cofigurative society.

To explore the dispositions privileged in pedagogies geared toward developing design literacies, we focus on the stories, practices, and products of *digital media producers* (e.g. designers of video games, community activists, documentarians) for several reasons. First, *digital media* are more than a means of 21st century communication; they shape what is produced and what producers do to foster new values and practices. Moreover, digital environments are increasingly pervasive, providing fresh spaces for students to learn design sensibilities. Second, despite the fact that digital media *producers* are the ones constructing everyday spaces that encourage pre- and cofigurative learning cohorts, there is a surprising dearth of analyses of professional producers, people at various stages and with different roles in the production process. Interviewing and shadowing these producers reveals the idiosyncrasies in how producers develop "new ways of learning," yet collectively the idiosyncrasies capture the rich, diverse ways that macro social, economic, and communicative shifts become materialized in everyday local practice.

Within these idiosyncratic stories, producers share striking patterns that reflect an expanded understanding of the places and practices of literacy learning, most notably the call to produce. This call has a long, if unacknowledged, history: as Aristotle argued about techne, it is through producing that people develop a richer understanding of a topic that they cannot get in another way. Producing, we argue, helps people develop the dispositions to problem solve in innovative ways, a hallmark of today's prefigurative generation that must make meaning in today's rapidly changing, digitally mediated world. Since design-based habits of thinking and ways of acting shape production choices, developing design literacies, we argue, is essential.

*Design Literacies* focuses on four dispositions that were common among the producers we interviewed: redesigning available materials from across many knowledge domains in innovative and responsive ways; being creative, often when working in new participation structures and in ways elders could not have imagined in years past; communicating ideas persuasively to a variety of people; and materializing an idea through multiple modes, modes elders have not historically privileged. Across these dispositions, producers talked about the need to collaborate with people from many knowledge domains and to be comfortable with ambiguity and even failure—inevitable and often valuable components of learning—while still committing themselves to achieving their desired goals.

To understand these dispositions, we opted to go to multiple sites where such design practices are evident: communities; schools; and, most distinctly, the marketplace. As youth spend more time in media-rich environments than they do in school, it seems clear these generally market-driven environments become "sandboxes" where youth develop innovative skills and orientations that productively rework traditional understandings of literacy within contemporary contexts. Consequently, by shaping 21st century products and practices that will become conventionalized ways of dealing with fleeting opportunities and trenchant challenges—in other words, problem solving—producers of digital media, in many ways, set the terms for learning. Understanding the machinations of design and the stories of today's producers offers an important look at those shaping 21st century education, an education that needs to prepare future producers to lead in the information age. Our hope is that teachers will take up the research we offer and apply it to their own contexts.

In this chapter, we set the stage for our study with the goal of showing how important the logics of digital media production are to our understanding of design literacies. We begin by establishing the need to examine digital environments—pervasive sites that are shaping contemporary understandings of learning and literacy. After taking stock of how two trends in literacy research, the social and semiotic turns, play out in these largely Web 2.0 worlds, we introduce the people central to this study. We end the chapter with an overview of the book, identifying key dispositions and themes we will explore in subsequent chapters.

## Literacy and learning in a Web 2.0 world

In exploring literacy and learning within Web 2.0 worlds, we quickly discovered that terms like "new media," "multimodal," and "digital media" are contested not only by our participants, but also by the theorists who have informed our work. Indeed, these terms mean different things depending on context and audience. "New media" seems more expansive, yet this capaciousness indexes how the definition of the term varies widely. For some, new media need not be digital media; rather, it can include using any traditional media in new ways. For others, like those with whom our interviewee Carrie Davis (pseudonym) worked, "new media scholarship equals humanities databases" (2008), a definition we find far too limiting. The term "new media" evokes further confusion when it comes to dating: Was it new in the 1990s, or is it new today? The disagreement among practitioners, confusion among our participants, and ambiguity about when exactly new media was new discouraged our use of this term.[3] Similarly, "multimodality" was not a common term for our participants, particularly those outside the academy, even though all those we interviewed explicitly used multimodal media to engage audiences in the reception, use, and reproduction of their work. Moreover, whether or not they worked in digitally distributed spaces, the producers we interviewed focused on issues of distribution associated with mass media in ways that are not captured in the term "multimodal."

We prefer the term "digital media." For us, digital media includes a focus both on the tools or means by which people participate in diverse environments and on an analysis of how these tools are part of larger shifts affecting the ways we make, understand, and distribute knowledge. These digitally mediated tools design environments where new forms of communication and learning can encourage embodied participant engagement via literate activity. Like Jim Porter, we, too, feel that digital "carries cultural connotations and avoids the instrumentalism implicit in terms like 'computer' and 'Internet'" (Porter 2007: xviii). "Digital" turns our focus to "technology-as-cultural-space as well as technology-as-production-space as a virtual environment in which humans live, not just a medium through which they talk" (xviii). Thus, our use of "digital media" highlights how everyday digital technologies influence our cultural spaces and the ways people interact with each other in these spaces.[4] As educators, we are particularly interested in understanding how people learn in these interactions and environments.

Digital media include wide-ranging spaces and technologies, such as mobile phones, electronic games and devices, MP3 and digital cameras. In *Design Literacies*, digital media generally refer to Web 2.0 tools and their multitude of resources and communication technologies such as Facebook, YouTube, wikis and portals such as Google. Too often, people's literacy and learning in these generally extra-curricular spaces are not recognized nor reflected in school-based curriculum. As Ilana Snyder notes, "despite the claims in the print media, students' out-of-school literacy practices have been largely ignored in the literacy curricula" (2008: 164). The disconnect between students' engagement in digitally mediated spaces and their literacy experiences in the classroom can make schooling feel out of sync.

As opposed to examining the well-trodden and comfortable logics and dispositions of many traditional schooling environments, *Design Literacies* seeks to understand the emerging logics and dispositions of those designing innovative digital environments where many students learn to be problem-solvers in their everyday out-of-school literate activities. Challenging the perception that these sites have little value, *Design Literacies* argues that such contexts pervade many people's daily lives, habituating users/learners to ways of reading, writing, and composing in these and other settings. In short, the producers of these everyday digitally mediated worlds are highly relevant, setting the terms by which people develop their everyday literacy habits today. Learning more about the logic undergirding their production practices warrants our attention.

An example of one highly influential, and equally contentious, site of everyday digitally mediated learning is gaming sites. The educational electronic/game-oriented company LeapFrog generated $442 million in net sales for 2007 (Lenhart, Kahne et al. 2008: 3), and educational gaming is considered small time. In the United States alone, the gaming industry generated $19 billion in revenue in 2007 (Lenhart, Kahne et al. 2008: 1), many video games gross more than blockbuster films (Lenhart, Kahne et al. 2008) and other widespread media, and gaming's influence continues to grow. Similarly, in the UK, 2008 marked the first time that sales of games surpassed sales of music and of videos (Cellan-Jones 2008). For educators, it's not just the industry's financial success that makes gaming noteworthy, but also gaming's movement into bastions of literacy. For instance, library-sponsored "Gaming Nights" draw thousands of teens (Rich 2008a: 3), while in schools, game-design principles (e.g. instant feedback for users/students; graphic imagery in game/course materials) garner big funding from educational foundations, as is evident in the MacArthur Foundation's granting of over $50 million to such projects since 2006 (Lenhart, Kahne et al. 2008).

Given this investment, it may not be surprising that much has been written about the possible consequences of gaming. Sensationalized headlines span extremes from alternatively claiming that video games can be addictive and bad for children to arguing that video games are pro-social and good for children. Frequently, media representations present opposing sides of how educators view digital media, as captured in this *New York Times* article:

> Children like Nadia [one of the tweens/teens prominent in the story] lie at the heart of a passionate debate about just what it means to read in the digital age. The discussion is playing out among educational policy makers and reading experts around the world, and within groups like the National Council of Teachers of English and the International Reading Association.
>
> As teenagers' scores on standardized reading tests have declined or stagnated, some argue that the hours spent prowling the Internet are the enemy of reading—diminishing literacy, wrecking attention spans and destroying a precious common culture that exists only through the reading of books.
>
> But others say the Internet has created a new kind of reading, one that schools and society should not discount. The Web inspires a teenager like Nadia, who might otherwise spend most of her leisure time watching television, to read and write.
>
> (Rich 2008a)

Despite these simplified binary representations of educators' views, popular media's coverage of youth engagement with gaming and other digital media has helped ramp up educational organizations' generally slow integration of digital media in the classroom, with varying responses. Doomsayers argue that games normalize anti-social behavior, promote gender stereotypes, and, perhaps most upsetting to teachers, distract youth from disciplined activities like reading. According to a report published by the Kaiser Foundation (Roberts et al. 2005), teens spend more time playing console and hand-held games (49 minutes/day) than they do reading magazines, books, or newspapers (43 minutes/day). In contrast, those promoting games' virtues explain that games can be used for positive ends, such as promoting educational content and orientations and encouraging the social networking needed in today's 21st century interconnected world (cf. Beck and Wade 2004). Moreover, as described in *The New York Times*, game supporters argue that games can act like a "gateway drug" to reluctant students, getting them involved in reading in a way they have not done in the past (Rich 2008b). This camp encourages schools' adoption of technology and even the buying of virtual islands for learning in the online world of *Second Life*.[5]

Instead of staking out a position on gaming per se, we believe that a more productive stance is to argue that digital media (and gaming is but one of its prevalent forms) is here to stay, and youth are embracing it wholeheartedly. Already, 97% of US teens have played video games (Lenhart, Arafeh, Smith, and Macgill 2008), and texting, IMing, and all sorts of other digitally mediated literate activities are similarly popular. These facts, for us, shift the conversation away from whether or not digital media are a good idea and toward the goal of making sense of, and possibly shaping, the role of digitally mediated communication in people's lives.

To facilitate this shift, however, requires us to define what counts as literacy in digital environments, another contentious issue. Part of the debate surrounding this issue is captured in a recent report by the Pew Internet and American Life Project (Lenhart, Arafeh, Smith, and Macgill 2008) entitled "Writing, Technology and Teens." This report highlights what researchers consider a paradox: although teens write extensively with electronic text and are "embedded in tech-rich worlds," teens see this use of symbols as fundamentally different from the writing they do for school. Digital media scholars Pamela Takayoshi and Christina Haas (2008) find a similar paradox: like students, teachers do not consider the hours teens spend everyday engaged in textually-mediated literate activities such as IM and email to be writing. Such disconnects have prompted Richard Sterling, chair of the advisory board for the US National Commission on Writing, to ask "How can we connect the enthusiasm of young people for informal, technology-based writing with classroom experiences that illuminate the power of well-organized, well-reasoned writing?" (Pew 2008). Since we believe that digitally mediated spaces can be powerful sites of educational innovation—capturing students' attention, encouraging peer-to-peer learning, fostering spaces for students to be readers and writers, and connecting students to others far and wide—we would reframe Sterling's question as a warning: given that digital environments provide such compelling sites for understanding innovation in learning and communication, educators would be ill advised to disregard, or denigrate, teens' digitally mediated worlds.[6]

One of our interviewees, Bob Camp (pseudonym) shares our desire to learn more about the possible value of contemporary digital media practices. As the developer of a gaming degree at a two-year community college in the Northeast United States, Bob explicitly focuses on gaming's value within educational settings:

> This is where I think games really stand to benefit us in education. The world is made up of complex, interlocking systems. You can't pull one strand without having an impact on the other strands, and sadly, the media likes to slice and dice things like, "Well, what do you think about this? Oh, you think that? Then that should be this way." Systems dynamics doesn't work that way. Because of the complexity that we have, we need to have a more complex way of dealing with and analyzing these problems. And games like *Sim City* and *Civilization*, even some of the shooter games [do] . . . Ultimately, I think games can become tools for a more complex thought process. I think that's what excites me about them.
>
> (2007)

Bob argues that games can encourage learning; by asking players to investigate the interconnections and complexity of problems and possibilities, digitally mediated games can help students learn to deal with ambiguity, synthesize diverse information, and analyze the interaction of many factors. And yet, despite how clearly Bob feels digital media warrant attention as important learning environments,[7] implicit in the quotation above is the belief that he must justify the value of gaming and game design. *Design Literacies* accepts that justification and seeks to examine both these learning environments and the stories of those who are shaping them in order to glean what educators can do in their own classrooms to foster similar learning outcomes.

## Effects of the social and semiotic turn
## for digital media literacy

*Design Literacies* builds on research from the last few decades' social and semiotic turns, research that asks us to reconsider how we define literacy. The social turn's largely ethnographic research broadened understandings of where literacy happens (i.e. not only in school) and showed literacy to be a social practice and not solely a cognitive one, the reigning idea in the 1970s. The semiotic turn opened up textual formats to include the multiple modes we naturally invoke as we communicate in our everyday, as exemplified when people use gestures or draw pictures when they talk through a story (Cazden 1988; Hymes 1996) or depict a family car (Kress 1997). In the 1990s, these social and semiotic turns came together, prompting researchers to examine a wider range of places and texts in their investigation of what it means to be literate.

The 2000s continued to expand definitions of literacy as evident in a pro-liferation of studies that posited an epistemology of plurality (in New Literacy Studies: Baker 2010; Coiro, Knobel, Lankshear, and Leu 2008; Knobel and Lankshear 2007; in Multiliteracies: Chandler-Olcott and Mahar 2003; Cope and Kalantzis 2000; and, in Digital Literacies: Beavis 2008; Carrington 2008; Davies and Merchant 2009; Lankshear and Knobel 2008; Snyder 2002). One strand of this plurality argues that we should value the globalized world of mul-tiracial, linguistic diversity instead of insisting on the value of only a singular, national language (Cope and Kalantzis 2000). A second strand of this plurality posits that literacy is not only alphabetic print, but inclusive of multiple modes. These and other studies in nested fields continue the social and semiotic turns, finding students' life worlds to be far richer sites of literacy than their school worlds. In the process, they expose the limitations of school-based definitions of literacy (cf. Alvermann 2006; Dyson 1993; 1997; Guzzetti 2009; Hagood 2009; Lewis and Fabos 2005).[8]

*Design Literacies* extends these research traditions. By looking at the ways pro-fessional digital media producers are defining what it means to be literate, *Design Literacies* investigates how a greater range of people and spaces are shaping the ways students develop valuable learning and literacy skills.

## *The social turn*

The social turn reflects a shift away from seeing literacy as a decontextualized cognitive skill of decoding symbols and toward seeing literacy as a highly situ-ated event (Heath 1983), practice (Street 1993; 1995), or activity (Prior 1998) in which people read and write in certain ways to be part of particular com-munities (Barton and Hamilton 1998; Gee 2003). As a cultural, social activ-ity, literacy is something people do. This interdisciplinary social turn is evident in anthropological and ethnographic research where literacy and learning are tied to out-of-school community practices (Street 1993); in educational research that highlights "funds of knowledge" (Gonzalez et al. 2005) or the complex and extended networks that families and students bring to literacy learning (Farr et al. 2009); and, in humanistic studies where a resurgence of narrative theory explores how the stories people tell about reading and writing reflect embodied, situated, and community-informed expectations (Brandt 1995; Journet in press; Wertsch 2002).

Throughout these studies, literacy is defined as a set of social skills—ways of participating with larger communities. This definition challenges autonomous views of literacy that posit a lone learner or a solitary genius; it also asks edu-cators to move away from over-valuing "original research" and move toward teaching effective ways to remix existing information to help students better meet today's opportunities and problems (see chapter 2). This definition also calls for a change in the particular structures that shape learning, away from hierarchical, transmission models and toward more peer-to-peer participation structures that facilitate meaning making (see chapter 3). Finally, this definition hints at how people of all ages have been tacitly apprenticed into these ways of thinking and acting without explicit and critical instruction; such an argument delinks education and formalized learning contexts, namely schools (Lave and Wenger 1991; Scribner and Cole 1981).

The separation of learning from schooling is also prevalent in today's Web 2.0 movement. For Kathleen Yancey (2004), this decoupling harkens back to the eighteenth century when significant changes in the material conditions of reading—most notably the technological shift that made affordable books available to the masses for the first time—meant that people were learning to read outside of schools. Today, according to Yancey, another technological shift—namely the widespread opportunities for people to publish largely through web-based possibilities—means that people are writing and publishing as never before. Indeed, as Deb Brandt (2008) argues, for the first time we may be a community of writers as much as we are a community of readers. This writing generally happens outside of school in digitally mediated spaces that cross a range of social, economic, and political contexts (cf. Marsh 2005).

Despite researchers in the social turn tradition having expanded definitions of literacy to include ways of participating in larger communities, literacy research in these extensive sites has generally focused on the practices of *users* in such communities (Chandler-Olcott and Mahar 2003; Cope and Kalantzis 2000; Hagood 2003; Jewitt 2006/2008; Knobel and Lankshear 2007; Kress 2003; Lewis and Fabos 2005; Moje 2000). As necessary and important as this research is for understanding contemporary literate activities, it is only part of the picture. Less examined are the perspectives of *producers*, those designing deliberate, if tacit, ways of thinking and habits of seeing through their design of digital media. Focusing on producers, *Design Literacies* extends research into the social turn of literacy studies by analyzing those shaping the literate activities and dispositions emerging in everyday digital media contexts.

### *The semiotic turn*

Similar to the social turn's recognition of the expanded contexts where literacy learning occurs, the semiotic turn recognizes an expanded range of modes (e.g. audio, visual, gestural) prevalent in everyday digitally mediated composing. This semiotic turn highlights that although text remains a central, even a privileged, mode of communication, text-only is no longer sufficient in today's digitally rich world; being literate across multiple modes is expected for successful contemporary communication (see chapter 5). And, although diverse composing modes are not unique to this moment,[9] the prevalence of such diversity represents not just a difference in degree but also in kind. Consequently, people need to develop what Stanford Mass Communication professor Henry Jenkins calls "transmedia navigation" or "the ability to deal with the flow of stories and information across multiple modalities" (2006: 46) so that people can read and write "across available modes of expression" (48). Such a call appreciates both that multimodal, digital composing is pervasive and that this pervasiveness has implications for the logics undergirding literacy learning, logics educators today need to understand.

Part of this appreciation is the acknowledgement that multimodal composing responds to and is part of large-scale social, technological, and economic changes. Organizations such as the National Council of Teachers of English (NCTE) make similar claims, calling teachers to locate their local teaching practices within larger contemporary contexts:

> Global economies, new technologies, and exponential growth in information are transforming our society. Today's employees engage with a technology-driven, diverse, and quickly changing "flat world." English/language arts teachers need to prepare students for this world with problem solving, collaboration, and analysis—as well as skills with word processing, hypertext, LCDs, Web cams, digital streaming podcasts, smartboards, and social networking software—central to individual and community success.
>
> (2007: 1)

Noting that work is only one of many arenas in which students should be prepared to lead, we share NCTE's claim that educators must respond to the both local and global contexts if we are to teach our students to succeed. These contexts value traditional pedagogical goals (e.g. analysis) even as they redesign these goals to better meet the possibilities enabled by multimodal composing environments.

For many teachers, preparing students to be leaders within these multimodal, networked environments is an issue of social justice (New London Group 1996; Selfe 1999). Like reading and writing for print-based literacy, reading and composing in digital spaces work to the advantage of some, generally those already with power (cf. Kolko, Nakamura, and Rodman 2000), but to the detriment of others. Those who have not developed the skills, attitudes, and comfort gained by critically engaging in the "new form of the hidden curriculum" (Jenkins 2006: 3)—how to participate in networked ways of connecting to others, to information, and to shared ways of making meaning—will be at a disadvantage in their futures, whether that is in school, civic forums, personal endeavors, or the workplace. To counter this disenfranchisement, schools should be centrally concerned with "creating the learning conditions for full social participation" (The New London Group 2000: 9–10), which includes designing and participating in multimodal networked environments. *Design Literacies* examines producers who are already modeling what is entailed in preparing people to be full participants in such environments.

11

### *The social and semiotic turn toward production*

An emphasis on production permeates both the social and semiotic turns, particularly within the Web 2.0 participation movement. Production challenges the sufficiency of static understandings of mono-modal academic literacies because, as Pamela Takayoshi and Cynthia Selfe argue, "In an increasingly technological world, students need to be experienced and skilled not only in reading (consuming) texts employing multiple modalities, but also in *composing* in multiple modalities, if they hope to communicate successfully within the digital communication networks that characterize workplaces, schools, civic life, and span traditional cultural, national, and geopolitical borders" (2007: 3; emphasis in original). Production, which includes Takayoshi and Selfe's notion of composing, also encourages people to use their literacy skills in a manner that exceeds a prevalent way to participate in contemporary culture, that of being a consumer. Drawing on Steven Heller and Veronique Vienne's (2003) *Citizen Designer: Perspectives on Design Responsibility*, Susan Hilligoss and Sean Williams are among many educators who seek to make students aware of and counter these limiting consumer-based options: "we must stop inadvertently training our students to ignore their convictions and be passive economic servants. Instead, we must help them to clarify their personal values and to give them the tools to recognize when it is appropriate to act" (2007: 230). Teaching students to produce their own ideas can meet this goal since production asks people to redesign given resources to better meet the needs of particular communities.

Many students are already engaging in multimodal composing and producing in their everyday lives outside of school. Report after report (e.g. Blau 2005; Lenhardt and Madden 2005) highlights how "we are moving away from a world in which some produce and many consume media, toward one in which everyone has a more active stake in the culture that is produced" (Jenkins 2006: 10). In digitally mediated spaces, a majority of youth are already active producers, with 57% of American teens being media creators (Lenhardt and Madden 2005); recent user-friendly production possibilities means that this percentage has surely increased. Seeking to understand the new dispositions people are developing as they participate in, and possibly redesign, the changing world around them, *Design Literacies* makes production a central focus of analysis.

## The people of *Design Literacies*

In presenting the stories, practices, and logic of media producers, we argue that this deliberate, deft work of choosing, making, revising, and converging digital, often networked, environments is best framed in terms of design and the development of design literacies. "Producers" is a term our interviewees were comfortable with, though production often has a mechanical association, an association we want to avoid. Design better captures the responsiveness needed, the nimbleness of thought and deed that enables people to rework given resources in innovative ways. Hence, throughout *Design Literacies*, we speak of producers, those making the action, who engage in literate activities.

Two groups of producers are central to this book: the producers we interviewed, and the producers we are. Below is a description of each, discussing
who the participants are, what they do, and how they work to create learning
environments that inform 21st century educations.

### *The producers we studied*

Instead of hearing abstract stories about generic "design literacies," we wanted
to hear a variety of perspectives that could enrich the numerous international
research studies that look at how digital media and digital technologies have
transformed literacy (Alvermann 2002; Davies and Merchant 2008; Jewitt
2006/2008; Snyder and Beavis 2004), but often with little to no account of how
producers did their work. If we rely solely on such studies, we miss the important
but seemingly idiosyncratic ways social, cultural, and economic forces are materialized in the everyday practices of learning in and out of school settings. We miss
the unexpected "telling stories" (Sheridan et al. 2000) that complicate flattened
descriptions of how these macro forces play out in individual lives; we miss how
innovative learning happens from the perspectives of individual people living it.

To get such detailed perspectives, we opted for an interview study, believing
that talking to producers and analyzing the practices and agendas that shape
their productions would allow us to tease out the dispositions most effective for
problem solving in digital environments. Primarily, we conducted interviews in
person but sometimes on the phone and, in two instances, via email. For some
participants we also conducted day-long shadowing and for all participants we
analyzed documents they shaped both before and after the interviews to better
understand their descriptions. In the end, we focused on 30 producers of diverse
digital media (websites, online games, film) for a range of audiences (children,
youth, adult programming) with diverse national backgrounds (see Table 1.1).

As Table 1.1 indicates, our definition of producers is quite encompassing,
sometimes changing with the number of participants and the role(s) each takes.
For example, some producers are individuals who oversee the entire process
from idea to completion, as is the case of the producer of award-winning documentaries, the designers of video games, and the creator of the Art for Autism
project. Some producers are part of a team, where one person may provide the
vision for the entire company while another may oversee one aspect, such as
the CEO and the director of marketing for the gaming company KumaGames
or the founder and executive producer of PBS's much-lauded *Reading Rainbow*.
Some producers play discrete but important production roles in international
companies, as evident in an editor at CNN or the director of new business
development and emerging markets for the music distribution company eMusic.
Regardless of the particular role or the size of the team, these producers share
the ability to solve problems by making an idea into a multimodal reality, distributed across wide networks in ways that call people to engage. This problem-
solving disposition toward contemporary meaning making defines a producer
more than any one specific practice.

13

*Table 1.1* Producers in this study

| Category or person | Description (nationality) |
| --- | --- |
| *Community hub members* | |
| Patricia Mavo | Founder of and web designer for Oral Heritage Project (American) |
| Warren Beavis (pseudonym) | Media consultant for Save Our Sisters, domestic violence shelter (American) |
| Diedre McCarthy (pseudonym) | Music CD producer, primarily of community artists (American) |
| Sarah Robbins | Community activist for local Indiana businesses, academic, and author of *Second Life for Dummies* (American) |
| Amanda Zadroga | Founder and digital media designer for ArtistsforAutism.net (American) |
| *Educational institution affiliates* | |
| Bob Camp (pseudonym) | Designer of gaming degree at US community college (American) |
| Carrie Davis (pseudonym) | Professor of new media/editor of leading online academic journal devoted to digital media composing (American) |
| Rebecca Haines (pseudonym) | Developer of first educational program in media literacy at The Harvard Institute on Media Education (American) |
| Rachel Hurdley | Documentarian/graphic designer (British), ESRC-funded project with B. Dicks: *Watching, Listening, Reading, Clicking: Representing Qualitative Research in Different Media* |
| Joel Madden (pseudonym) | Academic with digital media focus/newspaper columnist (American) |
| Kate Malone (pseudonym) | Digital media scholar working with academic team on www.mypopstudio.com, a website sponsored by the US Government to teach girls media literacy (American) |
| Ted Rogers (pseudonym) | Digital media scholar (American) |
| Gregory Stein (pseudonym) | Computer specialist for a graduate school of education (American) |
| Jake Telluci (pseudonym) | Digital media scholar (American) |

*Industry professionals*

| | |
|---|---|
| William Ashley (pseudonym) | Graphic designer (British) |
| Robin Benger | Documentary film maker, often for activist causes (e.g. importance of Nelson Mandela; the hazards of video gaming) (South African) |
| Kim Cartesh (pseudonym) | Sponsorship director for *Family Guy* website (Canadian) |
| Colleen Fahey | Director of marketing and audience development at Star Farm Productions (American) |
| Maggie Fern (pseudonym) | Website designer for educational books (Canadian) |
| Jose Garcia (pseudonym) | Production marketer for *Nick Junior* (Puerto Rican) |
| Jonathon Gravings (pseudonym) | CNN editor (American) |
| Robert Hammer and Alan Katsky (pseudonyms) | Illustrator and author of children's books (online and print work) (British/British) |
| Steve Kortrey (pseudonym) | Director of new business development and emerging markets for eMusic (American) |
| Cassandra Mathers (pseudonym) | Marketing director for *Club Penguin* websites (Canadian) |
| Twila Liggett | Executive producer of *Reading Rainbow* (American) |
| Paul Taylor (pseudonym) | Founder of Lawthority/computer programmer/ inventor (Canadian) |
| David Thompson and Ken James (pseudonyms) | Director of marketing and CEO of Kuma\Games (Canadian/American) |
| Megan Laughton | Producer at Chorion, focusing on adopting *Olivia* book series for television (Canadian) |
| Kasey Wong (pseudonym) | Graphic designer (Canadian) |
| Yling Yung | Anime and manga designer (Korean) |

After initial interviews with people who fit these criteria, we followed a modified snowball sampling where participants recommended other producers in both related and quite different fields. As researchers, we conducted interviews at times together and at times alone, yet always shared our data. For most participants, we use pseudonyms but some requested we use real names for them or their companies as a sort of payback in publicity for their time. Following the tradition of academics who give back to those who help their research, we've honored these participants' requests, and note this identifying information in Table 1.1 and in individual chapters.

In order to see if producers in similar circumstances share patterns in their design practices, we sought out producers across three domains: communities, education, and industry. Frequently, producers worked in more than one of these domains, providing useful comparisons. Whereas research on educational and community producers has been sporadic, research on industry professionals has been particularly scarce. Rebecca Haines (pseudonym), the developer of an educational program in media literacy at The Harvard Institute on Media Education, highlights two reasons for this absence, reasons others noted as well.

The first reason is that academics live within rigid disciplinary walls that have trouble accommodating digital media producers' interdisciplinary focus. Early in our interview, Rebecca describes her desire to reach audiences beyond the academy as a way to feel that her work is making an impact on the world:

> I got tenure in 1993 based on my traditional academic scholarship, which was, you know, refereed journal publication. I think my biggest article at that time which I got a prize for from the International Communication Award, got published in the best journal in the field of communication. I think maybe, and I am not kidding Mary, I think maybe fifty people probably read it and got it and found it valuable. And so I remember sitting on the beach at Cape Cod one summer, my children were small, and there I was kind of like, "what am I going to do with the rest of my life [now that] I have tenure?" I'm watching the big ocean lap against the shores and it's like here I am on the margin right, talking to an audience of nobody about something that really doesn't really matter, isn't really going to change the world in any way. So do I want to get out in the big wide ocean and get in the boat and get tossed around? And that's what I decided to do.
>
> (2007)

This happy narrative of engaging the big wide world, however, became more complicated as Rebecca describes academics' assessment of her engagement.

One complication is what Rebecca describes as academics' "wacko" insistence on viewing disciplinary boundaries as "silos" that discourage interdisciplinary conversations—a move Rebecca has struggled against throughout her career. According to Rebecca, academics' disciplinary training differs from digital media producers who engage with complex opportunities and problems, practices that call for a breadth of knowledge that does not fit easily within disciplinary categorizations. Producers of digital media need to be knowledgeable across disciplines. Even in larger teams where participants can specialize to some degree, to be a producer—a problem solver who shapes the vision and creates participation structures to accomplish this vision (e.g. garner funding, attract participants, design interface, market the project)—requires working across knowledge domains as diverse as English, marketing, graphic design, finance, early childhood education, new media studies, and communication. For Rebecca, this breadth is a large part of why digital media producers are unseen or institutionally confusing to many academics, who remain locked within disciplinary boundaries.

The second reason for an absence of research on industry professionals, according to those we interviewed, is academics' mistrust of those who work with industry. Rebecca describes this as academics' knee-jerk reaction against other academics working with people in business,[10] a belief born out of her experience. When Rebecca collaborated with The Learning Channel to create films that emerged out of her Harvard summer classes, Rebecca's colleagues "totally slammed" her as a "sell out." Rebecca continues, "In fact, if you Google me, you'll see 'Rebecca Haines sells out'" (2007). Challenging these hurtful comments that imply she gave up her beliefs to pursue this project, Rebecca relays how all sponsorships, even partnerships, require "a kind of negotiation," and she argues she was very aware of the issues at play:

> I went in eyes wide open, Mary. I knew what the strategic goals of this project were; it was part of [The Learning Channel's] sales marketing initiative. No corporation does anything out of the goodness of their hearts. There's always a catch to a strategic initiative and the question is, can their strategic goals, and your strategic goals ever line up. And in this case they did.
>
> (2007)

In this case, Rebecca found that *her* strategic goals of encouraging teacher education for those who could not afford the time or money to attend summer institutes were met. Instead of reaching perhaps 50 people through an award-winning article, these films reached thousands of people for years and years.

Others share Rebecca's account of academics' mistrust of those working with or in the marketplace. Acknowledging the danger of adopting industry goals wholesale for the classroom,[11] our academic interviewees argued that academic–business partnerships can help academics reach audiences far larger than anything they could dream of through traditional academic methods, such as a refereed journal article. Thus, like Rebecca, these producers were confused by other academics' antagonistic stance.

Unfortunately, suspicion in the relationship between those in academia and in industry goes both ways. Whereas academics may fear losing their mission to a business goal of creating consumers, many in industry seem to find little value in many academics' projects.[12] The producers we interviewed were exceptionally gracious, but several who opted not to participate seemed to feel either that academics spend more time talking than acting or that producers' participation may bring bad press to the company. The CEO and the director of marketing at KumaGames, both of whom spent hours with us while we shadowed them at their worksite, said as much. The director of marketing explicitly stated that most learning happens outside of school and that schooling is not part of the "real world," implying that academics were largely irrelevant to the "real world." Moreover, both these producers and a CNN editor stated that academic–industry partnerships would better students' education because these "real life" experiences include situated, embodied practice in addressing complicated everyday issues where learning how to problem solve was essential, a practice these interviewees reported was missing from their education. These producers highlight that many in business may not want to give up their valuable time for academics to research their practices. Despite academics' seeming irrelevance, some interviewees nonetheless seemed cautious of us, or perhaps cautious of the power of the pen, as evident in the KumaGames marketing director's asking, before he would address the informed consent form, if our research was going to appear in subsequent *New York Times* expose articles. This dismissal/suspicion combination makes access to the learning practices in these settings difficult for educators to access.

Whatever the reason, the lack of research on digital media producers indicates how too many academics have problematically ignored these thick networks outside of school settings that function as educational satellites to what we do. These satellites often take over as sites of meaning making more than schools do (cf. Yancey 2004), illustrating Allan Luke and Annette Woods's observation that "the achievement of literacy is produced by complex social, cultural, and economic forces—of which schooling, curriculum, and pedagogy comprise but one" (2008: 490). Given the statistics about how pervasive digital media are in the lives of our students, the producers of digitally mediated educational satellites are setting at least some of the terms of contemporary literacy practices. Academics' disregard for these satellites limits our ability to understand such sites of innovation that are shaping, and are shaped by, our students.

This lack of access is our loss. For example, in the last few years, business has exploited Web 2.0 possibilities where people openly and freely share information across global networks to make meaning collaboratively. Businesses use this collective wisdom to solve problems (e.g. fans-turned-producers) or develop new possibilities (e.g. viral advertising in audiences-turned-consumers) (cf. Tapscott and Williams 2006), often by creating networks that "tap the participation of large-scale social communities, who become invested in collecting and annotating data for other users" (Jenkins 2006: 50). In this process, businesses, among others, have learned the importance of developing communities that create and share information, a move echoing lessons of the social turn in literacy studies. Although this shift in who is producing information lessens the traditional gatekeepers' role, it increases the need for people to develop the skills and dispositions to engage critically with this shared information, a point several of our interviewees addressed. *Design Literacies* is invested, then, in examining how innovative digital media producers develop a culture of participation that encourages others to become critical meaning makers in communities where they evaluate, produce and distribute information across geographic space and time.

*Opening the black box*

To understand our interviewees' logic, the justification for their design choices, we draw upon Bruno Latour's (1987) concept of black boxing. Black boxing is when a controversial idea or process becomes naturalized and therefore no longer controversial. According to Latour, "The word black box is used by cyberneticians whenever a piece of machinery or set of commands is too complex. In its place, they draw a little box about which they need to know nothing but its input and output" (1987: 2–3). A common example of how a concept becomes black boxed is evolution. For years, most people outside of perhaps some religious communities no longer found the theory of evolution contentious. Rather, this at-one-time highly controversial scientific belief had become naturalized as fact. It's only when the black box is opened that we once again see how unresolved these supposedly stable issues can be.

Interested in the construction of scientific knowledge, Latour focused on understanding how complex issues and histories of scientific facts or technical artifacts are lost as they become translated into a homogenized stable thing. To open a black box and to examine the contentious and often contradictory nature of a field of knowledge such as science is to focus on "science in the making" and not "ready made science." Wanting these messier but more accurate understandings, Latour argues that scientists should "go from the final products [static, after-the-fact narratives] to production [messy, in-the-action processes]" (Latour 1987: 21) by examining the unstable and varied influences before they become explained away.

It is this focus on the messy processes of production, on how wide-reaching and often unwieldy practices become normalized, that is most relevant to our discussion of design literacies. Seeking to document the complex tensions digital media producers face before these become conventionalized and the alternatives lost, we investigate the beliefs and practices of digital media producers across different domains, looking particularly to find shared ways of orienting toward problem solving, ways that might have important lessons for educators. To address such a project, we seek to understand the messiness of, modifying Latour, production-in-the-making as opposed to production-already-made. Examining the actual practices of everyday digitally mediated producers, *Design Literacies* analyzes embodied examples that can enrich our understanding of the design literacies shaping contemporary sites of innovative learning, meaning making, and problem solving.

## *The producers we are*

A second set of producers who are important to understand are we, the authors. Jennifer is a Canadian, educated in the UK and currently teaching in an education department in the US. As a multimodal scholar, Jennifer brings expertise in researching the production practices of print-based publishers to our examination of the production practices of digital media producers. A specialist in community literacy, Mary P. is a writing studies scholar situated in an English department in the US. She has taught writing in community literacy centers, high school, community college and university classes, in New York and Chicago urban schools, in the US Midwestern farmland, and in the rural interior West of the United States. Coming from different countries, disciplines, and teaching backgrounds, we clearly value getting out of our national, disciplinary, and professional silos.

Like our participants, we needed to learn how to enact our production. Initially, we came from different angles to our shared interest in learning more about what we felt were changing definitions of literacy needed today. For Jennifer, our project comes out of her earlier research where she investigated how British and Canadian textbooks, as dominant curricular and pedagogical technologies, instantiate notions of literacy, education, even citizenship. Arguing that textbooks carry traces of social practice that disguise subjectivities, agendas, and eclectic discourses and ideologies that inform teaching and learning, Jennifer's research calls for greater dialogue between business in schooling and schooling in business. For Mary P., our project emerges from her research (2008) with community groups invested in making social change. Analyzing the logics embedded in everyday documents, Mary P. wants to understand how people can draw upon and compose a greater range of options for themselves as they seek to redesign the local and broader forces shaping their lives. For both of us, the production practices of people's everyday documents, especially with digitally mediated documents, have become rich sites demanding more attention.

Based on our desire to understand the digital media documents and the logics of those producing these documents, we registered for what we consider a 2008 digital media production boot camp at Ohio State University under the teaching, guidance, and mentorship of Cynthia Selfe and Scott DeWitt. To complete the boot camp, participants at this Digital Media and Composition (DMAC) two-week institute read some theory (e.g. Cope and Kalantzis 2000; Kress 2003; Selfe 2009; Takayoshi and Selfe 2007); experimented with genres of representation; designed and created digital media documents; and discussed issues inherent in being a multimodal producer, such as issues of access, equity, and agency. The capstone experience of the institute was the creation of a digital media project. Jennifer opted to create a film about our research project entitled *Literacy as Production*, while Mary P. chose to do a two-minute "pitch flick" for her school's graduate program in writing studies.

We had several goals in mind when we signed-up for DMAC. In addition to pragmatic benefits like being able to work together in the same room or go for walks together to sort out our ideas, we wanted to live in the shoes of producers, learn literacy practices implicit to digital design, and, ultimately, produce more sophisticated digital media. And yet, despite our extensive research in digital literacy, we quickly found out, like Paul whose words open this chapter, that it is one thing to read and even write about digital literacy, but it is another thing entirely to *think* like a digital media native, especially for us, when so much of our academic training has been fixed by written text.

Our DMAC learning curve was high, but essential for our work with *Design*

*Literacies.* We began our productions in ways that seemed appropriate: story-boarding our respective movies; listing existing visual, audio, and digital assets which would be combined to make the film; making new assets (Jennifer interviewed other producers to gather more voices of professional producers and Mary P. was interviewed to create the voice for her graduate program narrative). Nonetheless, our productions quickly ran into trouble, reflecting how we still privileged a print, alphabetic, linear logic. Jennifer watched as visual images of words problematically dominated her movie. Mary P. realized that her visuals should carry more of the weight and her voice-over narrative need not be omnipresent. For both films, the logic did not emerge from the most apt mode for that situation, or moment in time (cf. Kress 1997). In essence, we recognized that the first versions of our films were a flop. To shift our thinking, we needed to understand our messages within a complex matrix of the possibilities and limitations of how modes worked with and off each other. In the end, we revised our projects, making our films perhaps not the consummate statement about digital design but, if assessed on their multimodal salience, coherence, and structure (Selfe 2009), representations of competence no longer driven by monomodal print logic. The films reflected the multimodal practices and epistemologies of budding digital media designers.

Despite this important start to our own digital media design practices, we, like the producers we interviewed, had to overcome obstacles in order to make *Design Literacies* a reality. Production of this book meant living 1,800 miles apart, each working on individual chapters (Jennifer on chapters four and five; Mary P. on chapters one, two, three, and six) yet collaborating on a shared inquiry to understand the design literacies favored by digital media producers.

Similarly, we had to learn to negotiate a true spirit of interdisciplinarity as we moved across a wide range of theory (e.g. rhetorics of science, actor-network theory, ethnography of education, multimodal studies) not only with each other, but also with our imagined audiences. In this latter role we acted as what Karen Lunsford (in press) calls an "information broker," a concept borrowed from social network analysis that analyzes how people interact with others. As Lunsford describes, an information broker has "contacts with more than one cluster of people [in a network]; he or she controls the flow of information from one part of the network to another." Seeking to act as information brokers across disciplinary networks of people who study digital media, we discovered, sadly, there are too few models of this interdisciplinary practice—a fact that we feel deafens researchers to the rich possibilities of putting into conversation well-developed theories across multiple disciplines.

Finally, like the people we interviewed, we had to be open when our collaboration led us to unanticipated conclusions. One such conclusion highlights a problem with description. As we looked for producers' shared habits of mind and ways of being, across disciplines and domains, in and out of the academy, this study exposed the difficulty of explaining the various networks pulled into this complex project of digital media design.

21

Unfortunately, current depictions of innovative digital media design are rather impoverished, particularly when interdisciplinary scholars (e.g. from writing studies, education, film, communication, art, computer science) and community members and professionals from various fields (e.g. social services, activists, scientists, documentarians, consultants, law, marketing) come together. Too often, non-native digital producers invoke the logic and language of textual literacy/alphabetic print to describe the logic and language of other activities (e.g. digital media design), usefully constructing an order that is familiar and yet, in doing so, potentially misrepresenting or limiting what we see because we do not understand and, thus, cannot represent these activities in their own logic systems (Wysocki and Johnson-Eilola 1999).

Articulating the practices and dispositions of digital media producers can help build these connections, in part by illustrating interactions useful for encouraging others to understand and innovate on producers' logics. As Elizabeth Daley, Executive Director of the Annenburg Center for Communication and the Dean of the School of Cinema-Television at University of Southern California, argues, "certainly not all work in a discipline will be understandable to those without training, but for interdisciplinary work, faculty must find a language to speak across the boundaries. Multimedia may well have the potential to provide a much-needed new space in which cross-disciplinary conversation can occur between the humanities and the sciences" (Daley 2003: 36). Examining the ways digital media designers talk about their production can expose the tacit assumptions embedded in the discourses and practices of these digital media producers. We draw upon designers' talk and practice to help us articulate a language that describes common dispositions producers shared, dispositions we encourage educators to adapt as they think about their own teaching.

One complication to developing a language of description is the fact that our research highlights that even those proficient in action may struggle to talk about their practices and the logic guiding those practices. Many younger participants in this study are digital natives with implicit understandings of the logic of innovative production; this logic is embedded in the texts of their worlds, guiding and materialized in the design practices they encounter most days. However, despite their design abilities, these producers are often unable to articulate their dispositions and even their practices. In fact, few of us to date have a language that captures the production logic of innovative digital media design. As scholars and researchers of digital media production, we believe such a shared language can help us understand and foster contemporary problem-solving dispositions without, as is the case currently in many schools, overly privileging alphabetic print, thereby simplifying or excluding the logic and affordances of digital media production. Paralleling James Paul Gee's (1996) ideas about defining literacy, where fluency comes from both a tacit understanding that guides actual production choices and a meta-language that describes linguistic choices, *Design Literacies* examines the tacit and meta practices, including language practices, of digital media producers across a range of diverse sites. In the process,

*Design Literacies* aims to expose tacit and meta-level patterns that make our interviewees fluent digital media producers so that educators can adopt similar patterns in our classrooms.

## Chapters: setting the stage

The logic of digital media producers is quickly informing everyday interactions; therefore, we seek to understand producers' practices and develop a heuristic that describes and analyzes the logic that undergirds these practices. Doing so can encourage people to develop a meta-awareness of this production logic and an ability to shape this logic through their own engagement with digitally mediated texts and environments. This, in turn, can help people understand the design literacies central to today's prefigurative world.

As language and literacy scholars, we are particularly interested in highlighting patterns, what we are calling dispositions, that form the basis of this language that captures what we mean by design literacies. We describe what we consider to be core dispositions, that, although generally tacit, mark shared practices the producers we interviewed used to problem-solve. The following chapter descriptions detail the dispositions we found particularly salient.

Chapter 2, "Practices and language of design," focuses on the core disposition of design, the tacit strategies digital media producers develop when they take readily available resources and make something new that better matches the designers' needs (New London Group 1996). This chapter focuses on two clusters of design practices: remix, where producers combine found things (e.g. a clock radio and a bean bag); and, convergence, where producers combine functions/networks into the same things (e.g. bundling products from Twentieth Century Studios, Target stores, and Altec speakers for better distribution of eMusic). These practices highlight, first, how innovative thinking has less to do with original creations and more to do with creatively combining existing resources and, second, how we need a language to describe producers' practices and dispositions so that novices and experts can better understand their own and others' innovative work.

Chapter 3, "'Fearless creativity': participation structures and sponsorship in dense media networks," focuses on the disposition of creativity. This chapter argues that, if we want to develop creative people prepared for today's challenges and opportunities, then we need to design environments that encourage creativity. These environments, or architectures of participation, call participants into certain relationships with people and practices of making meaning. Digital media are providing opportunities to rethink traditional architectures of participation in ways that, we believe, can encourage innovative thinking. Despite this promise, we caution that the increasing commercial influences of participation on the web are re-shaping people's readily available opportunities to act—whether in digitally mediated spaces or elsewhere—in ways that educators can both learn from and rework to better suit their purposes.

23

Chapter 4, "The art of spin" focuses on the disposition of spin. Spin is a way of describing the shaping of content, and overall it does so through modes of expression (chapter 5). Exploring how four producers of digital and televisual texts transform a set of ideas and principles into multimodal compositions, this chapter argues that spin can be a contemporary substitute for print-based logic of composition. Print logic alone does not cover the kinds of skills students have at their disposal from extensive digital media use and, ultimately, print logic does not suffice for multimodal composition, the primary means of modern communication. Consequently, we argue that policy and pedagogy need a language and logic that depicts the kind of creative outside-of-the-box thinking that happens when designing media.

Chapter 5, "Modes spinning stories" extends the art of spin, design, and re-design by focusing on the dispositions producers have when they select particular modes to materialize discourses, agendas, beliefs, and so on. Words, photographs, sounds, and interactivity express ideas in nuanced ways, and the story of three producers and the choices that they made during production highlights dispositions that are fundamental to making meaning with 21st-century texts. Examining how and why producers selected particular modes-in-texts, we extend research in the area of modal choice (Mavers 2007), by providing three studies that offer thick descriptions (Geertz 1996) of how decisions are made. Based on these case studies, we argue that by focusing on modal choices, students can analyze not only their local texts but also the larger concept of how particular modes afford meaning. Such fine-tuned analysis of multimodal composition fosters critical awareness of current text content design as well as anticipates possibilities for future texts that students will create.

In the conclusion, we investigate what educators can take away from these shared dispositions of new media producers. Knowing that there are many dispositions digital media producers share and knowing that any enactment of these lessons will depend on the local conditions, we still argue that teachers can better reach their students and improve their pedagogies by taking into account the practices and logics of current digital media producers, who are invested in teaching their users. Based on these case studies, we argue that teachers can reach their students through what we consider key dispositions for design literacies.

In the "Afterword," James Paul Gee looks back into the distant past, in order to detail how our study with digital media producers exposes long-standing epistemologies and frameworks of language production that have largely become naturalized and therefore rendered invisible. *Design Literacies* investigates the enabling and policing of these language practices. Consequently, *Design Literacies* can help educators understand their own and their students' practices. The goal of this, as Gee points out, is for educators to teach people to make wise choices about their language practices so that people design "a better, more humane, more sustainable world."

# 2

# PRACTICES AND LANGUAGE
# OF DESIGN

There's an encouraging element [about the possibilities of design]
because William Gibson said, "The street makes its own use for
things" and it's about how when technology is in the hands of
people, they will often just do things with it. And even with the
iPhone, the moment it came out, it got hacked and people tried
to make applications for it, and were unlocking it. With every
update Apple makes, there's a new fix on the other side. There's
this sense that technology does not ultimately determine us.
People work against it and remake it. Maybe that comes from the
same sort of design-your-own-doll-skills [that girls may develop
playing with online sites]; maybe years later, those [early skills]
become, "hack the iPhone" . . . [So] you take skills from the sandbox and you go somewhere else that wasn't supposed to be the
sandbox, and you make it your sandbox. One of the keys is the
skills, and then you apply them in whole new contexts.

(Jake Tellucci, digital media scholar, 2007)

In the last decade, "design" has received a lot of attention in the academy, perhaps most notably since the New London Group's 1996 manifesto "A Pedagogy
of Multiliteracies: Designing social futures" but certainly in more recent mani-
festations as well (e.g. Cope and Kalantzis 2000; Kalantzis and Cope 2005). In
this pedagogy, people use the resources of meaning currently available (available
designs) to create new resources (the redesigned). The process by which people
do this work is called "designing." Contrary to a reigning academic theory of
critique that seeks to point out the flaws of existing structures, the New London
Group's theory of design advocates a process of altering available designs to
create new resources that better meet current conditions; across its diverse
enactments, design promotes problem-solving dispositions that elicit flexible,
creative reworking of givens to better suit 21st century possibilities.

As the opening quotation illustrates, the ability (even inevitability) of everyday
users to remake existing things and practices is a central goal of design. One example of this designing is "remix," a set of practices where people combine or

rework existing artifacts into something new. Diverse remix practices are perhaps best known for their role in pop culture production, and the opportunities for these cultural productions reflect the technologies available in making particular remixes. In recent decades, for example, new recording possibilities have helped musicians and DJs "sample" or "sequence" parts of songs into new compositions. More recently, digital "mash-ups" have remediated various modes (e.g. text, image, sound, video) into a new and different, if derivative, whole. And, although some may argue music sampling or digital mash-ups are reserved for a few, by 2005 already 25% of American teens had sampled and remixed media (Lenhardt et al. 2005); that number is surely growing as user-friendly technological opportunities to remix have increased.

Moreover, tens of thousands of people take advantage of remix possibilities through forward thinking corporations like Creative Commons, "a nonprofit organization that increases sharing and improves collaboration" by encouraging people to, as its tag line indicates, "share, remix, reuse—legally" (Splash page n.d.). Musicians, visual artists, designers, and authors contribute to such sites, celebrating the easier and greater distribution of people's work. This widespread distribution facilitates remix possibilities and other forms of digital media creativity because "innovation and new ideas come from building off of existing ones" (Creative Commons "Spectrumofrights comic 1" n.d.). Remix's call to locate innovation in a process of reworking available resources rather than in a unique creation extends far beyond pop culture. In fact, according to digital media scholars Johndan Johnson-Eilola and Stuart Selber (2007), remix is becoming a standard practice in a range of academic disciplines, from film to architecture to web design.

While Jake discusses remix practices, other producers we interviewed privileged different design practices, such as those affiliated with convergence. Convergence has become a buzzword, generally meaning the ability to bring disparate ideas and things together, often to create new practices. Convergence can, for example, mean the consolidation of physical businesses, linking seemingly disparate products: physical books joining with eMusic give us downloadable Books on Tape. In the context of *Design Literacies*, however, we use convergence or convergence culture to address media convergence, where old and new media interact in undetermined, but nonetheless highly influential ways. For Stanford media theorist Henry Jenkins, media convergence is both a means and an end to influential changes: "convergence culture represents a shift in the ways we think about our relations to media, that we are making that shift first through our relations with popular culture, but that the skills we acquire through play may have implications for how we learn, work, participate in the political process, and connect with other people around the world" (2006: 22–23). Convergence culture encourages people, often playfully yet significantly, to expand how they understand and engage with the world. Like remix, convergence may be most visible in pop-culture artifacts but the practices enabling and enabled by these convergence practices encourage innovation far beyond that realm.

Both remix and convergence focus on combining instead of on seeking a pristinely unique creation. Whereas remix privileges blending existing artifacts, convergence privileges uniting functions and therefore linking previously dispersed networks. What these and related design practices share is the idea that design is a problem-solving practice, where people reuse available resources in new ways that better meet producers' goals. Design, then, is less a prescribed series of practices than it is an orientation toward engaging with the world and making it more to one's own liking. This orientation takes many forms across multiple channels but coheres around practices that bring together the affordances of old and new media in unanticipated ways, eventually reshaping available materials to create something new that better suits current needs and opportunities.

The self-directed, innovative design sensibilities encouraged by Jake and other producers differ from many traditional school-based pedagogies, which privilege original ideas over redesigned resources for cultural production (e.g. think about anxieties over plagiarism or individually-focused assessment). Although some current theories account for design practices such as remix and convergence, too often teachers miss the complexities of redesigned cultural production that do not map neatly onto the stable patterns or existing grammars so often taught in school. The ability to negotiate emerging design opportunities, however, is a recurring disposition found among the producers we studied and is a disposition students should develop in schools, if students are to engage fully with the problem-solving possibilities they will surely encounter in their future, if not their present.

To better understand these design complexities, this chapter investigates the practices and languages of description from three producers' perspectives with the hope that this investigation can encourage more innovative pedagogies. First, this chapter contextualizes two key design practices, remix and convergence, and examines how producers use these practices. Second, this chapter analyzes producers' language, highlighting how impoverished our descriptions of digital media design are. To develop a better language of description, we adapt James Paul Gee's (1996) argument that people gain fluency with language acquisition by developing their tacit skills and meta-level awareness; in this chapter, we capture both how designers naturalize ways of acting and knowing in digital media environments (i.e. tacit abilities) and how designers talk about their actual practices (i.e. possible meta-understandings). Uniting these goals, this chapter examines the work of those engaging in innovative digital media design—whether in the community, market, or academy—in part by articulating their theories of design; in part by analyzing how these theories are operationalized in practices, such as remix and convergence; and, in part by exposing the need to develop a language to describe these practices.

## Case studies: the activist, the businessman, and the scholar

Drawing from the many participants who described their production practices in relation to theories of design, this section analyzes the stories of three digital media producers: Amanda, an amateur, activist producer with sophisticated design sensibilities that far outpace her ability to describe her production processes; Steve, a business professional who explicitly locates design within macro social and economic changes that create opportunities for new products and partners; and, Jake, an academic who is atypically articulate about how individuals work with and against larger social forces shaping design practices. Although their practices and language often differ, these producers, like so many of those we interviewed, find the practices of contemporary design central to their work. Examining the ways producers talk about their work exposes common design practices among those addressing the problems and possibilities they see around them.

### *Activist designs: Amanda Zadroga of Artists for Autism*

During the time of our face-to-face interview, Amanda Zadroga was a soon-to-be college graduate who most overtly matches the idea of a producer, having created websites that attracted wide audiences since her tween years. As a digital native, Amanda has long been "writing the web," a movement where, as of the year before our interview, everyday people were creating web-based content so rapidly that they were doubling the size of the web every six months (Educause n.d.). In her design, Amanda tacitly understands the importance of media convergence for users and producers in digital media environments, offering a model of how convergence culture provides the impetus for her literate activity and shapes the diverse ways she materializes her activist desires. Despite being a model of how people enact convergence, Amanda struggles to articulate this understanding. This struggle highlights the need for a language of description of digital media practices for digital natives, as well as for less experienced people trying to understand and engage in digital media practices.

Just prior to our interview, Amanda had taken Rhetoric of Activism, a class Mary P. taught in the spring of 2007. This class investigated contemporary trends in activism, in part by focusing on the recent changes in the rhetoric and practice of what a *New York Times* series of reports was calling "philanthropreneurs" (Strom 2006). Students started this class by learning discourse analysis methods and then examined how representations of contemporary activism in newspaper reports, grant proposals, and strategists' white papers enabled and constrained activist agendas. There were two major assignments. The first was a seminar paper that analyzed the rhetoric of one activist trend or organization of the students' choice. The second assignment was to create a document or portfolio that "did work in the world," a task that asked students to make what they had learned meaningful for a public audience (e.g. compose a grant proposal, zine, newspaper article, website, audio essay).

Students did wide-ranging work. One English Education major wrote, illustrated, and self-published an environmentally focused children's book to fill a void she saw in the classroom where she was student-teaching. Two spoken-word poets compiled their own work as well as solicited poetry from the people at the places where they volunteered (Elijah's Promise soup kitchen and a domestic violence shelter) to make a collection they sold at their poetry slams; the funds these two students raised went back to these organizations.

Amanda's project was as powerful, but it did not always seem that way. A quiet student, Amanda seldom volunteered to speak in class, fumbled a bit when called upon, and proceeded haltingly through her oral presentation. And yet, this presentation of self did not capture what Amanda could do, as she made clear in her final project and in our follow-up conversations about how she could advance her project in the future. Amanda decided to create a website for people with autism who were turning 18 and, therefore, were about to lose their supportive New Jersey state benefits. When asked why she wanted to do this project, Amanda replied:

> Well, I originally wanted to do something with music . . . I don't know, so I tried to find something that was more, I don't know, something that might be brought to action. And I chose autism because my two cousins are autistic and my brother is developmentally delayed so it's something that hits close to home . . . And so I wanted to incorporate [my autism website] with music because I think it's a good way to get people involved versus just having the website.
>
> (2007)

When thinking about how to engage a public audience, Amanda used sound, text, and images to call her audience to action (see chapter 5 for a fuller description of the power of multimodal choices). In fact, as a digital native, Amanda found digital media to be a comfortable way to express her interests for much of her life. At age 13, when Amanda was in 10th grade, she designed the MetsRock.com website, which, according to Amanda, received over 1,000 hits a day. After her New York Mets baseball phase, Amanda became more involved in music and created a fan site (weerez.com) for the nationally touring band Weezer. Among the many fan sites for this band, Amanda's was the most popular. She paid over $60/month to host this site, created several different layouts during her webmaster tenure, and provided what she believes is "every single piece of Weezer media ever. Every single song: B sides, rare ones, live, bootlegs, and like all the videos and things like that" (2007). Her work earned what she considers the ultimate compliment: Weezer's manager described her site as the "Weezer fans site titan." To back up the compliment, the band linked to Amanda's site from their home page.

Although Amanda eventually sold this site and turned her attention to other interests, these early projects proved useful training grounds—the sandboxes of Jake's opening quotation—to hone her design sensibilities. By the time she was in college, Amanda had developed enough traditional rhetorical skills (e.g. attention to audience) and digital rhetorical skills (e.g. attention to a digital aesthetic, navigation) to know that new technologies produce new types of designs and affordances in the use and production of documents. For example, the convergence of previously dispersed material (e.g. baseball statistics, bootleg music) can encourage the development of grassroots communities that shape their own messages and the larger, more official communities to which they are linked.

As Amanda delved into her autism project, she realized that, for her work to be meaningful in affecting change, it needed to be nestled into diverse networks of people, texts, and organizations. And although her goal remained consistent, rhetorically Amanda needed to create and manage various pitches about her work across these networks. By the end of the semester, Amanda had compiled a collection of artifacts that made up her Art for Autism project.

In addition to her project's website (see Figure 2.1), Amanda created a CD (including designing the CD and the digipak), an email soliciting the participation of New Jersey bands, a letter to branches of Barnes & Noble and other stores asking them to sell her CD, book shelf markers and a shelf card for Barnes & Nobles, a Public Service Announcement aired on the radio, a poster, a sales letter for a booth at a charity golf outing and an autism educational night at a local disability center, letterhead, and business cards. Supplementing these documents, Amanda made herself the object of publicity, including articles in the local *The Home News* and *The Star-Ledger*, radio pitches on Q104.3, and reviews of her album in various print and radio forums. Amanda was finding

*Figure 2.1* Home page for ArtforAutism.net

a way to be visible in, if not fully saturate, the media, and these ancillary texts helped make her project meaningful beyond the requirements for the course.

To make her texts effective, Amanda not only selected distinct modes for particular documents; she rhetorically, responsively, situated her representations across diverse distribution networks, highlighting how local concrete design practices manifest the projection and coordination of complicated, distributed networks that may not be readily apparent. From emailing bands to partnering with Barnes & Noble, through websites, music CDs, solicitation letters, and community posters, Amanda worked across multiple media channels and rhetorical registers, linking various aspects of her Art for Autism project in a highly generative manner. In the process, she both tapped traditional top-down distribution networks that amplified her ability to get her message out and relied on bottom-up, grassroots models to diversify her potential audience.

Despite her sophistication in practice, however, Amanda was unable to make her design sensibilities explicit. In fact, Amanda appeared at times to be *in*articulate both in class and in the interview. For example, Amanda said the phrase "I don't know" 49 times in one 45-minute interview. At times, this phrase functioned as a placeholder, almost the equivalent of "ummm." At other times, the phrase functioned like a tag question at the end of an utterance, like the more typical, "you know what I mean?" Most often, however, Amanda said "I don't know" when asked about why she thought something about design. For example, when Mary P. asked Amanda to follow up on her stated dislike of a particular website, Amanda replied: "Their links were, I don't know, they weren't out there. They weren't like 'this is this' and 'this is this.' You had to click on something and then I don't know. *Autism Speaks* is a good site if you want to look at it." While Amanda and Mary P. were in the same room during this exchange, they were not looking at a shared website, making it hard to know what Amanda's phrases such as "this is this" meant.

This lack of clarity is quite typical of this interview, as illustrated in another exchange where Mary P. asked Amanda to explain why she thinks in a certain way.

> *Amanda:* Well, I think visually. And, I don't know, I guess just some commercials, some ads are just really nice.
>
> *MP:* How are they "nice?"
>
> *Amanda:* They are just visually appealing. I don't know. They flow. They . . . I don't know. Well it depends. Some of them don't flow; some of them are choppy, but that works.
>
> (2007)

In this exchange, what makes commercials appealing is still unclear, especially since Amanda's description indicates that commercials "work" both when they flow and when they are choppy. Amanda is trying to explain a complex assessment of taste, no minor feat. Even so, as in other sections of the interview, Amanda does not (cannot?) articulate her assessment.

Talking with producers like Amanda exposes how tacitly understood practices of innovative design facilitate producers' abilities to problem solve. For Amanda, educating the general public and securing funding for adults with autism is her activist project, the problem she wants to address. Whether combining audio, visual, and textual elements in her own design or communicating across radio programs, newspaper reports, community posters, or bookstore displays, Amanda understands the importance of accessing the possibilities afforded by digital media. And yet, Amanda also highlights how even digital natives struggle with the same troubles so many non-native teachers of digital media do: we lack a language, maybe even a meta-awareness, to describe what we are doing.

Perhaps some do not need this meta-awareness; Amanda learned her design skills through extensive practice and with the guidance of out-of-school sponsors, primarily her cousin/close friend Katie, a graphic design student at a nearby college. Nonetheless, Amanda may be better able to communicate her ideas and perhaps even understand her work differently if she were able to develop a richer vocabulary and meta-awareness about design. And, while Amanda represents a growing number of people learning their digital media skills outside school, alone or with friends, few of us spend that amount of time and passion designing online sites and have trained sponsors able to help our voluntary digital media projects. Instead, for most people who are not in formal degree or training programs where such language may be overtly explained, learning design practices could be facilitated by having a vocabulary that indexes actual practices of digital media design.

Such a language—which would certainly include issues of convergence as well as other design practices—could help us think about prevalent designing practices and, hopefully, foster environments that would encourage innovation in digital media, the medium of the 21st century. As the following sections detail, some producers—usually older than Amanda and in professional careers that require them to explain their practices to novices—are helping to provide this meta-description.

### Convergence in consumer culture: Steve Kortrey and eMusic

Steve Kortrey (pseudonym), like many commercial producers, talks through his life with technology by alluding to his resume. He started working in the mid 1990s dabbling with online advertising while working for a North American advertising agency. Since then, Steve has explored digital marketing as part of the global team for Bertelsmann AG (#1 book and music seller) and then moved to Earthnoise, a precursor to YouTube. After running the digital media and eBooks group for McGraw-Hill, Steve spent a few years in marketing for Audiobooks.com and, at the time of our interview, he was the Director of New Business Development and Emerging Markets for eMusic.com, the second largest online distributor of music after iTunes. Like those in the *Wired* reports at the height of the dot.com bubble whom Barbara Warnick (2002) analyzed, Steve has fully ensconced himself in a wild-ride business model where people grab opportunity and money as they build a new "frontier." Steve's frontier is based in and mediated by digital media.

Given this digital media market framework, it should be no surprise that at eMusic Steve wants to map innovative ways of seeing and interacting with the world onto a closed, seemingly direct route that leads people to buy products. Whereas Jake, as we'll see, wants to open design processes that can disrupt top-down business models, Steve seeks to limit the range of recognized possibilities afforded by digital media within a market-driven logic. Within this logic, design must be highly responsive to change if a company is to meet and/or create opportunities afforded by these changes. For example, when thinking about how to market downloadable eBooks available at eMusic, Steve analyzes how, as bookstores connect or consolidate (e.g. Bertelsmann partners with Amazon and Amazon links to Audible.com), business practices must also change, whether by transitioning from physical artifacts (like books) to digital artifacts (like eMusic's downloadable eBooks) or by forging new collaborations. For those who "go it alone," Steve sees "tombstone after tombstone of retailers that have massive customer bases who have now tried to transition into the digital model and haven't done it well" (2007).

As Steve is well aware, when businesses adopt a "digital model," new relationships are formed between companies, markets, customers, and products. These relationships alter how media (e.g. physical and digital music and books) are produced and consumed and how businesses should operate in this climate. Within these changing conditions, Steve and other digital media professionals make digital media meaningful by naturalizing the ambiguity of people's changing relationships with artifacts and other people; they create familiar yet new products and practices that match people's expectations as well as market conditions.

To do this successfully, Steve thoughtfully investigates some of the exact questions we in the academy are wrestling with, such as, what does it mean to read, write, and listen today? Challenging static understandings of reading, writing, and listening as stand-alone practices, Steve argues that products like eBooks are part of larger activity systems. Within various activity systems inhabited by time-strapped, multi-tasking professionals, the consumer practices surrounding successful eBooks, according to Steve, are more like listening to the radio than reading. Listening, Steve argues, is preferable, since, in the dot.com mentality of super-efficiency, eBooks/books-on-tape can help people "time shift," turning supposedly "wasted" time like commuting into something productive like keeping up with "must *read*" books. Given the time constraints of busy professionals, this is a good selling point.

For Steve, the *what* of new designs (e.g. eBooks at eMusic) is integrally connected to the *how* of enacting these new designs (e.g. distribution of eBooks). This *how* has to do with convergence. As Director of New Business Development and

*Figure 2.2* eMusic "touchpoints"

Emerging Markets at eMusic, Steve hopes to black-box or naturalize new ways of reading, writing, and listening by bundling eMusic with other "touch points" that enable users to purchase songs with a mere touch of their hands (see Figure 2.2). To date, eMusic has over 100 active partners that saturate people's engagement with technology and normalize eMusic into peoples' emerging practices. For example, with AT&T's wireless products, eMusic becomes part of the phone; with retail stores like Target, Best Buy, and Circuit City, eMusic is part of their "digital music starter kit;" with New Line Cinemas and Twentieth Century Fox, eMusic is bundled with movies; with technology and hardware partners such as Altec Lansing speakers, eMusic can be linked with almost anything.

This partnering makes seemingly disparate products converge in ways that will naturalize certain practices—practices we couldn't have imagined just a few years ago. According to the practices encouraged by eMusic's touch points, consumers will not think about but rather adopt the provided business model, which will result in better distribution of eMusic's products. In this top-down, market-driven model, corporations provide the practices, products, and contexts that encourage people to express their agency through their purchasing power. Thus, successful digital media provide not only useful products, but also the networks that enable a product to be adopted easily and the discursive constructions that make this product desirable.

Charles Bazerman (2002) describes this process of linking complex networks in order to facilitate the adoption of a new technology in his analysis of Thomas Edison's production of the light bulb.

> For any technology to succeed (that is, to establish an enduring place within the world of human activities), it must not only succeed materially (that is, produce specified and reliable repeatable transformations of matter and energy); it must also succeed symbolically (that is, adopt significant and stable meanings within germane discourse systems in which the technology is identified, given value, and made the object of human attention and action).
>
> (335)

This "symbolic engineering" must be "established and maintained in many networks" (336). For Edison, this meant that the acceptance of the light bulb required the convergence and normalizing of multiple disparate realms, from the science of electricity to the attention of and acceptance by financial backers, the media, and a purchasing public, to name just a few.

The acceptance of today's digital media is similar. For example, the success of eMusic relies not only on technological advances that make new products, but also on the normalizing of rhetorical and material practices that make eMusic an accepted part of people's everyday lives. To foster this acceptance, Steve's symbolic engineering is a practice of design that successfully links and mixes, among others, discourses of innovation, capitalism, utility, and literacy. As Steve makes clear, business people are producing innovative digital media that are re-mediating conventionalized practice.

We can anticipate some lessons by once again looking at historical precedent, such as the impact of the technology of electric light. As Bazerman describes,

> the new technology of electoral light (and electrification in general) brought about major ruptures in the new way of life, creating new categories of thought and interaction, new organizational entities, new governmental procedures and bodies, new daily schedules, new products, and new dangers. Not only did it change meanings within existing discourses (see, e.g., Schivelbusch, 1988); it also created new discourse networks with new sets of meanings . . . Despite the great changes that came in the wake of the new technology, incandescent light and power had first to be built on historical continuities of meaning and value. It had to take a place within the discourse and the representational meaning systems of the time before it could transform them. Electrical light had to find representational terms that could be comprehended before it could create its own new world of experience and meaning.
>
> (2002: 349–350)

Bazerman's analysis illustrates how representations of Edison's electric light were part of large scale changes that shaped "new categories of thought and interactions." While eMusic is hardly as revolutionary as electric light, eMusic is but one of myriad technological developments redesigning today's society. These changes share much with Edison's time: new products, new categories of thought and interaction, new social organization, and new ways of life. As with Edison's time, these changes first appear and are made sense of within older networks, but, even during this initial phase, these technologies are part of new ways of experiencing and making meaning in the world, new ways to problem solve. To understand local uses of new digital media possibilities, we need to analyze both local artifacts and design practices, such as those evident in eMusic interfaces, and how such artifacts and practices are situated and naturalized in larger forces. These understandings can help us develop a language to describe the practices and dispositions new technologies may encourage.

### *Amateurs designing widgets for a larger community: Jake Telluci, digital media scholar*

Jake Telluci (pseudonym) is almost the same age as Steve, is also a white male, and views technology as central to his work. Yet, whereas Steve's entry into digital media has been primarily through his job, Jake's has been through personal exploration and play. Moreover, whereas Steve wants to black box market design choices, Jake wants to open these black boxes with the hope that people can redirect pre-packaged or top-down goals in ways not initially intended.

At the time of the interview, Jake was a newly minted Writing Program Administrator with strong digital media skills that he had learned and initially used almost exclusively outside the university. Jake played computer games in the 1970s and 1980s as a kid, and, as he grew older, the web became a way for him to meet men with whom he hoped to have romantic online relationships. While studying literature in graduate school, Jake discovered that digital media was an area he could pursue for his own scholarship, and he eventually completed his PhD with a dissertation on digital media. In an intensive digital media composition workshop (similar to the DMAC workshop Jennifer and Mary P. describe in chapter 1), Jake discovered a personal and professional community of digital media designers that has been central to his work in the field as both a producer and a teacher of digital media. And, while Jake only alludes to this in passing, it seems his production practices were enhanced significantly after his ongoing conversations initially with other producers and, later, with novices Jake mentored and taught.

As the following interview excerpts bear out, Jake can eloquently theorize the nature of design, an ability atypical of many other of our research participants, though perhaps less so of digital media producers within the academy:

I see the function of the academy fundamentally as to structure new knowledge, and I think *really good design produces its own kind of knowledge.* So innovative design is a new way of reading the world and seeing the world and interacting with the world and understanding the world and in the same way that new knowledge is . . . Like good research does not reproduce the research that was already done, *good design does not reproduce the design that was already done.* But it acts as the field. And in the same way, for me, the best theories are the ones that serve as useful tools for predicting reality. So a really good theory will let you know what's going to happen in a certain situation. *Really good design gives you new templates for mediating your design to the world.*

(2007, emphasis added)

Like other academic digital media producers we interviewed, Jake found design to be central to his work within the academy. Design balances theory (the investigation of conceptually challenging ways of understanding) with praxis (pragmatically acting to impact people's everyday). By mediating theory and praxis, design produces new knowledge; when design "acts as the field," it teaches people what to attune to, thus encouraging particular ways of knowing and habits of being.

Understanding design as a powerful lens that helps people make new meaning enables Jake to pursue his interest in online community building. When Jake talks about the promise of design, he particularly celebrates how amateurs can build local communities to redirect traditional access to power. Jake illustrates his valuing of the amateur and the spaces that encourage amateur participation not only in the quotation that opens this chapter, but also throughout the interview. For example, when he describes the trendy youth-targeted Chumby—a new "it" electronic device marketed toward youth culture that combines high-end technological gadgetry with low-end arts and crafts (see Figure 2.3)—Jake details how amateur engagement, and not necessarily professional sophistication, is shaping innovative design. In this description, Jake is less excited about the next new thing and more excited about how amateurs can take this new thing and create new dispositions or habits of meaning making. Jake is excited about the possibilities afforded by what he calls a "remixed culture."

I think we live in a remixed culture. The cutting edge of amateur design is not in what we think of as new media as in terms of websites, but in terms of *how do you take two different data sources and combine them into something entirely new.* You know, there's a new product out called Chumby. Chumby is a cross between a bean bag and an alarm clock. It's got a cute little screen and it's got this literal bean bag padding all around it, and it's wifi connected. It has a user-generated community of widgets. One of your widgets will get you the weather every morning; one of them will track eBay auctions; one of them will get

*Figure 2.3* Chumby surrounded by personal items

you latest movie reviews. That, for me, is where new media design is happening. Where people are creating new things, not in terms of colors, *but I think design is moving towards data elements or taking two things like eBay and flash and turning it into something new—a widget for a larger community*, if that makes sense. The fascinating thing about Chumby is that people can customize the Chumby with these widgets but that people can also customize their Chumby by bedazzling it. It's this high tech Internet appliance that's also inviting traditional, feminized arts and crafts.

(2007, emphasis added)

In Jake's discussion of a remixed culture, he combines both the promise of remix (e.g. the ability to bring together the seemingly disparate feminized crafts and high-end technology) and the promise of convergence (e.g. the ability to link, access, distribute, and even create knowledge in new ways: "you take two different data sources and combine them into something entirely new"). These bottom-up possibilities are guided by local users who innovate on existing designs to meet the needs of particular communities. Yet Chumbies are distributed by mega corporations, allowing for greater delivery possibilities. The potential of remixed design, therefore, is how it mashes both bottom-up amateur and top-down business forces.

Jake lauds this messy process where local users engage in do-it-yourself design that moves beyond merely adopting sleek, beautiful, and off-the-rack resources in order to design something new. This messy bottom-up pressure counters what Jake describes as an "Apple-Ikea-Volkswagen life"—a life represented by "three iconic interlinked businesses and communities that are all centered around a particular flavor of design" (2007). As Jake argues: "When most people think of design, that's [Apple-Ikea-Volkswagen] the design that they think about. But design is happening in these other Linux bean bag areas . . . They're not the cool kids like Apple. Design's getting ugly and that's exciting" (2007). Attending to both bottom-up grassroots practices and top-down industry practices, Jake looks beyond the sleek models that businesses provide to "ugly" models where amateur communities design interfaces that present information for others to use and normalize. And, when local users defy what Jake sees as the profession-alization of design that pushes amateurs to sanctioned "sandboxes" outside of the "real" work of making meaning, they facilitate local communities coming together and taking control of what innovation can become.

In these passages, Jake implicitly argues that digital media design offers par-ticular epistemologies that can facilitate innovation. As Henry Jenkins (2006) describes, "Ways of knowing may be as distinctive and personal as what kinds of knowledge we access, but as knowing becomes public, as knowing becomes part of the life of a community, those contradictions in approach must be worked over if not worked through" (44). Working through digital media design offers Jake the promise of new ways of knowing and acting that can encourage local communities to have a greater say in defining their wants and needs, in part because these local communities would then have greater control over the tools that help make and distribute information, even knowledge.

If, as Jake believes, design mediates our understandings of the world by shap-ing what we pay attention to and, therefore, what we come to know, then new design brokers new approaches to knowing that, in turn, rework existing design. Part of community-based new design requires a negotiation between top-down, often market forces that provide the established design/ways of knowing, and bottom-up, grassroots forces that encourage new designs/ways of knowing. As this local innovation becomes shared and accepted, it pushes on the normalized ways of knowing and doing, thereby creating different norms that, ideally, can extend beyond a local community.

## Conclusion

Amanda, Steve, and Jake provide snapshots of the current practices of amateur, entrepreneurial, and scholarly digital media designers, who identify and pursue contemporary challenges and opportunities that respond to evolving economic conditions, social practices, and ways of making and using knowledge. They do so by reworking available resources to help people make new meanings in and of the world. Across these three snapshots, Amanda, Steve, and Jake share a conviction that digital media design is a central process of creative problem solving within a changing 21st-century context. And, although the particulars of their design are guided by different contexts and problems to be solved, as a group the designers in this chapter raise shared questions: How do people use design to accomplish their goals? How do designers talk about this process? What do these practices and languages of description have to teach educators today?

As each of the producers in this chapter wrestles with how to use digital media to investigate, create, and distribute new information, artifacts, and practices, they return to the design practices of remix and convergence. In the process, they make routine new or controversial ideas and practices in order to encourage people to act in particular ways. Amanda uses media saturation or media convergence, where multiple media (e.g. radio, television, movies) become interconnected, making her project appear everywhere, as if it were an already accepted fact (cf. Prior et al. 2007). Steve, however, uses a different strategy to promote the use of his products; he facilitates consumers' choice of eMusic by black-boxing the selection process of eMusic products. Jake, meanwhile, wants to open up the black box of community resources so that everyday people remix and remake ways of being and knowing into artifacts that can be used to bolster a community from the bottom up. Using various design processes to engage in local ways of problem solving, these producers applied the design strategies of remix and convergence that future producers may then rework in the academy and in their community.

The cycle is complex, and the prevalent practices are diverse, making a way of talking about design vital, especially since few people have the tacit facility of a digital native or the meta-awareness that often comes through more formal training. Since the ways people talk about design shape what solutions they can know or share, this language of description should both detail producers' practices and examine how such practices naturalize new ways of being and knowing. Amanda, Steve, and Jake's practices and how they talked about these practices offer a start to defining the characteristics of such a language.

Throughout her activist project, Amanda highlights the need to attend to convergence and media saturation, even in local contexts, in order to get her message heard in a crowded marketplace. This digital native provides less explicit meta-description than Steve and Jake, but implicit in her design choices is the sense that multimodal, digitally mediated texts should provide many ways for an audience to engage (e.g. listen to music, email band members, buy CDs, learn about a topic), which, in turn, calls on producers to spread that message across multiple media. Based on our interview with Amanda, a language of description should detail multimodal elements of a document (see chapter 5) and the participation structures available to users who engage with these multimodal elements (see chapter 3) as the participants work with and across various media.

Steve describes design within capitalistic frames: professional contexts dominate; innovation is materialized in purchasing practices; black boxed design processes maintain a top-down business model; the promise of convergence responds to economic shifts. By attending to how markets put pressure on and create new possibilities for practices that once seemed static, such as reading and writing, Steve underscores how current literacy practices are located in multiple frameworks shaped by contemporary social changes—technologically with easy access to downloadable books on tape; economically with mega stores consolidating; socially with busy professionals multitasking to use their time more productively on commutes. Educators need to learn about, understand, and expose these frameworks, appreciating the possibilities they afford and working to redesign the frameworks where appropriate. In this way, Steve highlights how a language of description should be responsive to the discursive and material forces shaping digital media (e.g. capitalistic discourses), but, we add, this language should also create a space to embrace, critique, and/or work against, or perhaps at an angle to, these forces.

For Jake, the promise of digital media design is the possibility for amateurs and local communities to redirect power for their own ends, in part, as this chapter's opening quotation reminds us, by grassroots community users pushing against top-down business models. Like Steve, Jake believes that design decisions are based on epistemologies that are changing in the digital age, though Jake has a different goal. For Jake, digital media offer the promise of seeing, knowing, and acting in the world in new ways. This promise is evident in everyday products. People not only bedazzle Chumbies in a personalized manner, they also use Chumbies as "a widget for a larger community"—they create new resources for orienting to the world that might benefit their community. Local producers can encourage such innovative redesign by experimenting with new ways of knowing as well as of organizing and distributing that knowledge. And, while some may question whether modifying new gadgets like Chumbies represents new epistemologies, these are the sandboxes where people work out the epistemologies that undergird the practices digital media encourage. Moreover, the practices emerging out of these epistemologies won't stop at bedazzling; they will spill into the rest of our lives, affecting how we connect to others in civic, work, and personal interactions. Consequently, for Jake, too, a language of description scopes upward from specific practices to envision ways of being and knowing that foster the dispositions that lead people to action, to become problem-solvers in their world.

These broad suggestions of what a language of description may include—from the local articulations of multimodal practice to the general situating of these practices within overlapping discourses of redesigning the appropriate epistemologies—may prompt educators to promote practices that both remix available resources to better suit students' goals and examine how needed resources may converge across multimodal and dispersed networks. Pedagogies built on these design practices offer promising possibilities for preparing students for the changing conditions of meaning making needed in today's globalized context.

The goal of such design-based pedagogies is to develop dispositions toward problem solving (cf Johnson-Eilola and Selber 2007), a goal that academics and those in the marketplace share. The means of achieving that goal, however, are weighted differently. Whereas academics often push toward producing original research, the producers we interviewed used traditional academic skills (e.g. analyzing complex issues, synthesizing diverse materials) to combine existing resources (e.g. selecting appropriate communication modes) in order to innovate on existing possibilities. Acknowledging educators' legitimate concerns about design-based pedagogies (e.g. concerns of plagiarism and intellectual property violations), we nonetheless encourage teachers to tap the possibilities of design-based pedagogies that, as Michele Knobel and Colin Lankshear (2008) argue about remix possibilities, too often remain unfulfilled. Troubled by this outcome, we call upon educators to provide students with genuine opportunities to link existing networks of resources and practices in new ways so that students engage in cultural production. Such opportunities could teach students the "socially developed and patterned ways of using technology and knowledge to accomplish tasks" that Scribner and Cole define as the essence of all literacy practices (quoted in Knobel and Lankshear 2008: 28). Such lessons, the producers we studied point out, illustrate that design can play a central part of developing students' literacy dispositions in the 21st century.

# 3

# "FEARLESS CREATIVITY"

## Participation structures and sponsorship in dense media networks

> I definitely think there needs to be an emphasis on learners creating their own content. The whole Web 2.0 movement and the prosumer movement[1] put the means of production in the hands of everybody . . . So definitely [I support] that idea of prosumer education, of the instructor stepping aside and acting more as a travel guide and letting the students lead the way. And the kinds of things the traditional age students now, the kinds of things that they do for fun, the forms of media that they create voluntarily on their own time for fun. There is no reason why those forms shouldn't take prime center seat in the classroom . . . If we carry those kinds of philosophies that we are seeing from the technology culture into classroom, I think we are going to see really big developments.
>
> (Sarah Robbins, Second Life author and consultant, 2008)

According to Sarah Robbins—a PhD candidate with a new media dissertation, a media consultant to universities and businesses, and the co-author of *Second Life for Dummies* (2008)—educators need to develop innovative learning environments that foster greater student participation, in part by tapping the types of learning students are already doing. Modifying "prosumer" ideas popularized by Don Tapscott and Anthony Williams's best selling and optimistically proselytizing *Wikinomics* in 2006, Sarah believes that collaborative, open, and especially peer-powered knowledge-making participation structures can translate into 21st-century pedagogies as easily as they translate into the 21st-century business practices Tapscott and Williams advocate. These new participatory practices challenge educators to alter both what they are doing and how they are doing it.

Responding to this global educational challenge, Canadian-based Tapscott,

UK-based Williams, and US-based Robbins share a call to rethink what is valued in a rapidly changing world, an idea that seemed everywhere in the mid 2000s. For example, in another *New York Times* best selling book, *A Whole New Mind: Why Right-Brainers Will Rule the Future*, Daniel H. Pink (2006) argues that recent global changes call for new mindsets, ones based on creative thinking. According to Pink, global forces are pushing us into a new Conceptual Age where creators and empathizers will be valued: "We are moving from an economy and a society built on the logical, linear, computer like capabilities of the Information Age to an economy and a society built on the inventive, empathetic, big-picture capabilities of what's rising in its place, the Conceptual Age" (1–2).

The reasons for the emergence of the Conceptual Age are many: the abundance of material wealth has encouraged the aging Baby Boomers to pursue meaning as well as means; white-collar jobs are being offshored for a fraction of the cost; automated new technologies complete left-brain jobs better and more cheaply than people can. What unites these disparate trends is the fact that the once-lauded analytic abilities—skills Pink calls "L-Directed Thinking," because they are predominant in the left side of the brain—are no longer the prized skill. Although the L-Directed skills of analysis, sequential thinking, and logical reasoning will remain essential, they are "no longer sufficient. In the Conceptual Age, what we need instead is a *whole* new mind" (51), and this whole new mind includes traditionally devalued R-Directed skills, such as empathy, and pattern recognition, and holistic meaning making. According to Pink, in the Conceptual Age, creators, empathizers and those strong in R-Directed thinking will "rule the future."

Pink's call to see creativity—defined by the strengths of both analytical intellect and empathetic inventiveness—as a key 21st-century skill is just one example of how creativity is the new buzzword for the way people orient to knowledge, to others, and to opportunities/problems. Moreover, creativity is a valued disposition shared across the producers we interviewed. And yet, how are we preparing our children to engage in creative and innovative thinking when No Child Left Behind bubble sheets, A-Level exams, and SAT-type tests privilege left brain thinking? If globalized high stakes testing in schools seems out of sync with contemporary needs, how are today's students of all ages preparing for the demands of the 21st century?

One unlikely place is video gaming, a contemporary manifestation of creativity in design and in participation on a mass scale. Already, 97% of teens have played video games—a multibillion dollar industry grossing far more than other media (Lenhart et al. 2008). Moreover, video gaming is now a central component for mega book publishers, such as Scholastic and Random House, which commission games to coincide with the release of new books to draw youth into reading and to reach new markets; *Harry Potter* is now a best-selling book series and a video game, available in a variety of platforms to people in Australia, the UK, Europe, and the US.

The extensive voluntary participation in a variety of gaming environments, many of which teach about historical events or encourage reading and composing both on- and offline, raises important questions about what we can learn from gaming in relation to schooling. What thinking goes into games' media-rich ecologies that call people (producers and teachers; players and students; sponsors and schools and libraries) to participate in ways that may prepare them for the creativity they will need in their futures? What can the architects of these ecologies teach us about the texts and the participation structures prevalent in today's digitally mediated world? How do contemporary meaning making tools mediate the ways people learn to be active, creative knowledge makers in dense media ecologies? Answers to these and other questions can help educators better prepare students for the challenges they face.

In this chapter, we examine these questions by looking at several individuals involved in the production of games: Colleen Fahey, the Director of Marketing and Audience Development of a global children's gaming company, Star Farm Productions; Ken James and David Thompson (pseudonyms), the CEO and the Marketing Director at KumaGames, respectively; and, Sarah Robbins, the teacher, scholar, consultant, and author whose quotation opened this chapter. These very different game developers share the belief that online gaming can foster curiosity and creativity by tapping user-generated knowledge through what Daniel Pink would consider both L-Directed Thinking (e.g. analytic skills) and R-Directed Thinking (e.g. collaborative improvisation).

Based on our analysis of how these producers define and foster creativity— a key disposition among the producers in this study—we argue that, in order to encourage creativity, we need to develop environments that promote a range of ways to participate in creative endeavors. Sarah Robbins calls these constructed environments "architectures of participation" that elicit the creativity we seek in our students. In this chapter, we examine how new media producers develop these participation architectures within frameworks shaped by old and new sponsors and by Web 2.0 possibilities.

## Structures of participation

To examine how contemporary producers design creativity-friendly environments and participation structures, we adapt Jean Lave and Etienne Wenger's (1991) notion of legitimate peripheral participation (LPP). Lave and Wenger's research on LPP comes out of anthropological studies that decouple learning from schooling (cf. Scribner and Cole 1981). In these studies, researchers examined how people learn in everyday environments, often through apprenticeship models where more experienced participants of a community call new members into competency by ratifying them as legitimate participants with valuable contributions to make to the life of the community.

As Lave and Wenger argue, participation in these communities is the leading edge of fostering behaviors, attitudes, and knowledge-making. If, citing an example from our study, World War II buffs want to learn more about particular battles, they can become functioning members of World War II gaming communities, such as those offered (occasionally) at *Kuma\War*. As they learn the conventions of this community and offer their expertise in ways that are ratified within this community, they may come to different understandings of a particular battle, the world of gaming, or even the process of making meaning due to participation in the community of this game. In this chapter, we examine how people develop and modify participation structures through their involvement in these innovative online environments.

These environments are generally rich media ecologies that offer multiple ways to be a member of the community. Modifying Bonnie A. Nardi and Vicki L. O'Day's term "information ecologies"—"a system of people, practice, values, and technologies in a particular local environment" (2000: 49)—we argue that media ecologies are local environments of interlocking media where people, practices, and technologies interact.[2] The opportunities provided by these media ecologies encourage certain practices and discourage others. For example, children wanting to learn more about and even shape favorite television shows can go to particular websites and, in addition to watching past episodes of the show, can offer suggestions about future episodes, create a fanzine, and upload video essays about important episodes. And, while creating fanzines or suggesting plotlines for future episodes may be discrete activities, the participation structures across these activities often build upon and support each other throughout the site. Even if Nardi and O'Day's ecology metaphor seems to naturalize these highly constructed activities by evoking associations with the natural environment, "media ecologies" productively highlights the complex relationships between interconnected practices and people shaping local spaces.

The possibilities for online environments to change participation structures is evident in the way the web has changed from a provider of "flat" information (Web 1.0) to a connector in socially driven, locally made networks (Web 2.0). In a recent talk about Web 2.0, media communication scholar Henry Jenkins describes key characteristics of new forms of participatory culture where consumers take media into their own hands, rework the content to serve their own needs, and generate new material. The characteristics of this culture include:

- low barriers for engagement,
- strong support for sharing creations with others,
- informal mentorship where experienced people help newer ones learn technologies and social processes,
- pervasive belief that the peoples' contributions matter, and
- shared recognition that not all need to participate, but all are free to participate when they are ready (2007, "Authors").

In many ways, Jenkins's model echoes Lave and Wenger's construction of legitimate peripheral participation. Specifically, for a community to take root and for learning to be encouraged, there must be many opportunities for members

46

to contribute and be ratified by established members of this community. For example, if Sarah Robbins wants to encourage alumni to get involved in a university's *Second Life* island, she needs to construct environments and participation structures for "newbies" to shape their interactions with others in an inviting and supported way so that all members—new and continuing—feel valued and remain part of the *Second Life* community.

People find their way into these online communities via a range of sponsors. Deborah Brandt (1998) explores the idea of sponsorship in her investigation of the sponsors of literacy. For Brandt, sponsors are "any agents, local or distant, concrete or abstract, who enable, support, teach, model, as well as recruit, regulate, suppress, or withhold literacy—and gain advantage by it in some way" (166). In other words, sponsors are dispersed groups that "set the terms" for how people engage in a range of practices by offering incentives and disincentives that are often taken up in ways that obscure sponsors' influences. Adapting Brandt's definition, we find the sponsors in our study to be individuals (e.g. family, online communities) as well as institutions (e.g. The History Channel, a work place) that provide the essential support and serendipitous connections that enable the producers we study to advance their goals in some way. Considering that most sponsors of students' digital media literacy are not found within the university (cf. Carrington 2008; Yancey 2004) and, therefore, are often not acknowledged and/or understood in traditional classroom practices, our study of these diverse sponsors becomes all the more important.

As we will discuss further, online gaming sites such as the ones analyzed in this chapter illustrate how designers of Web 2.0 environments materialize today's valued participation structures. Creativity, both in the design and the use of these sites, is a central goal of these sites' architectures and is naturalized by old and new sponsors. Located within dense media ecologies, these constructed architectures encourage a variety of participation possibilities for people with diverse motives and abilities. Assessing how and why producers of these sites create particular participation structures will help educators understand what they may want to do in order to foster their own creative, successful classrooms.

## Case studies: the seeker, the gamers, and the architect

The following case studies examine how digital media producers encourage the creativity needed for 21st-century success. Within this larger project, we focus on how these media producers exploit the unique conditions of meaning-making in a Web 2.0 world in order to elicit people's creativity so that they can legitimately engage in their communities. Targeting children and adults, newcomers and experienced gamers, in educational and commercial settings, producers in these case studies provide sketches of what educators preparing students for current and future possibilities should address as they create appropriate learning environments for today's students.

Colleen Fahey, the subject of the first case study, works with and across different industries, projects, and people, coming to understand how a digital mindset is shaping people today. Tapping both her analytical and empathetic skills, Colleen is invested both in learning how to be creative in this digital mindset and in helping others, in this case youth, do the same. This case study highlights how fostering creativity for diverse users requires designing multiple ways to participate in this community.

The subjects of the second case study, Ken James and David Thompson, illustrate how online spaces integrate previously distinct groups in ways that can help educators think through the structures necessary to support dispersed, peer-driven education. In particular, these KumaGames executives highlight the importance and complications of courting new and old sponsors to make sense of online engagement.

Sarah Robbins, the subject of the third case study, is explicitly analytical when articulating her design of participation structures in online environments. Her "architectures of participation" encourage innovation across a range of contemporary peer-driven meaning-making spaces, exploring how Web 2.0 affordances can shape contemporary creativity. This case study helps educators imagine what architectures they can set up in their own classrooms in order to foster the types of creativity needed today in a range of settings.

These case studies individually and collectively examine what kinds of environments foster social engagements that encourage people to learn conventionalized and innovative ways to participate in and shape their surroundings. As we'll see, characteristics that encourage this learning include building structures that ratify a range of participation, tapping old and new sponsors, and situating contemporary meaning-making practices within and against pervasive Web 2.0, often market-driven, prosumer educational models.

### Seeker of multiple paths: Colleen Fahey of Star Farm Productions

Before becoming Director of Marketing and Audience Development at Chicago-based Star Farm Productions, Colleen Fahey had a long history in marketing, working accounts for Nestle, the US Postal Service, Target, and Purina Latin America. Eventually, Colleen focused on cultivating children's markets, and her accomplishments are known to billions around the world: for over 10 years Colleen headed the team that developed McDonald's Happy Meals, which, according to Colleen, now constitute 20% of McDonald's adult and children's markets. Colleen decided to work for Star Farm because she was attracted to what she describes as "the healthy creative environment," which "appealed to [her] emotional side," and because she felt Star Farm "got kids' engagement with technology" in a way that few others get, "which appealed to [her] intellectual side."[3] To paraphrase Daniel Pink, Colleen appreciates how Star Farm values a creativity that uses her whole brain, and this version of whole brain creativity is a central theme throughout Colleen's interview.

Star Farm presents its vision of creativity to the public through dense media environments that invite audiences, generally children, to participate, as articulated in Star Farm's one-minute "pitch" video. (About Star Farm video n.d.) The screen shot setting up this pitch video depicts the Star Farm logo as a backdrop to two foregrounded boxes. The neat rows of the background illustrate how the "farmers" at Star Farm Productions methodologically cultivate dreams, harvesting them for all to share. In the left-hand box, four Star Farm Productions gears work together to meet the needs of audiences from the cradle, to preschool, to tweens and teens, to college. In the right-hand box, cut out stars depict actual people, images from Star Farm products (books, shows, games), and global partners, making visible the connected, interactive stars nurtured by Star Farm Productions. Overall, these images balance the orderly, analytic work and the emotive, connective work that define Star Farm's creativity (see Figure 3.1).

Overlaying upbeat, slightly pulsing music that conjures energy and excitement, a female voice narrates Star Farm's message:

Today's digital generation lives in an explosion of media.

Kids both consume and influence media using online communities, mobile technologies, and new versions of traditional media.

*Figure 3.1* Frame from *About Star Farm* video

Unlike traditional entertainment companies that retrofit content, Star Farm's process has multiplatform reach and audience participation built in from the start [a cartoon character squeaks "Hello"].

Linking quality storytelling and audience generated content, Star Farm is building cradle to college relationships.

Star Farm's partners are global leaders in publishing, television, marketing, and consumer products. With world class partners onboard and many more on deck, Star Farm will lead the way to unprecedented opportunity in the new world of empowered entertainment [a boy, apparently playing with Star Farm products, exclaims "That's awesome"].

Star Farm provides multiple, multimodal ways for viewers to participate, from watching cartoons to generating online connections. Furthermore, in the video users are texting while watching television and creating videos while re-watching webisodes, thus highlighting that at Star Farm, children are encouraged both to consume and produce media. In this process, Star Farm does not retrofit 20th-century content and practices; rather, Star Farm uses 21st-century technologies and the participation practices afforded by these technologies to build relationships with users and global partners. The result: a playful engagement with contemporary storytelling, both in content and participation possibilities, that lasts from "the cradle to college."

According to Colleen, Star Farm's mission is centrally concerned with creating innovative environments that encourage others to participate and, by extension, foster their own creativity. This participation-focus is evident throughout the pitch video, where involvement with contemporary digitally-mediated environments is foregrounded. Such involvement in Star Farms properties fosters, according to Star Farm's website, "the creative spirit in kids from preschool to high school" (Properties page n.d.). While Colleen assumes many successful companies have the intellectual prowess to think through how to design engaging spaces that encourage children's creativity, she particularly values how Star Farm pursues this goal by developing dense media ecologies that encourage a range of participation structures in innovative and "unprecedented" ways.

*Designing ways to be fearlessly creative in rich media ecologies*

Star Farm seeks to foster fearless creativity by encouraging youth to participate in a range of experiences that allow them to pursue their goals. Star Farm not only creates spaces for people to take up fearless creativity; it foregrounds images that invite viewers to vicariously live what fearless creativity might mean. Star Farm's most overt representation of fearless creativity is *Edgar & Ellen*, Star Farm's first major "property." *Edgar & Ellen* "tells the story of highly intelligent, fearlessly creative twins who live in the sticky sweet town of Nod's Limbs" (Press Room n.d.). Edgar and Ellen see the world differently than the other citizens of Nod's Limbs. And, although their plans seldom work as they anticipate, these playful, inventive characters continually seek new ways of acting and being in order to bring about the changes they desire.

Edgar and Ellen's fearless creativity is central to these heroes, in part because the story designers want children to take up this creativity both in the world of Star Farm products and their own worlds. Like the main characters in this story, children need to understand and develop their own creativity and the website, according to Colleen, gives *Edgar & Ellen* audiences that opportunity:

> Children are a part of the creative process . . . And we want to encourage and foster fearless creativity in the children . . . That's particularly *Edgar & Ellen*'s domain. They are fearlessly creative . . . And one way that we do the TV thing [encourage creativity in the viewers of *Edgar & Ellen*] is that we have an online question, like 'Edgar is created as carrying three things in his satchel that he wants to make a prank out of. What are these three things?' Then they [the viewers] tell us three things. Then we choose a child's submission and credit the child by name.
>
> (2006)

In addition to encouraging viewers to become invested in returning to the program and the website (i.e. to see if their suggestions were chosen), such activities give people an opportunity to make something new that is valued by the community. For Colleen, the structures that invite participants to shape and be validated by their community are central to fostering creativity.

If Colleen is driven by the question, How do we create a world where participants stay fearlessly creative?, then her answer lies in the ways Star Farm encourages children to participate. Exhorting youth to "let your voice be heard" (Advisory Board page n.d.), the Star Farm site not only wants kids to engage in *Edgar & Ellen*'s "online community that serves as a hub of interaction," but invites audience participation, as the opening video explains, through multiple platforms and entry points that encourage children to engage both on and off the website. On the *Edgar & Ellen* site alone, people can participate by blogging, posting their art, uploading fans' videos (fans create their own episodes or recreate favorites), offering suggestions for future storylines (10% of *Edgar & Ellen*'s storylines come from viewers' suggestions), learning where to buy related merchandise (creative play is centrally linked to the distribution afforded by business partners like Target or specific bookstores), and becoming active in various Star Farm Boards (including the Kids, Parents, and Professional Boards).

As evident on the website, Star Farm locates *Edgar & Ellen* in multiple storytelling ecologies, each providing a range of participation structures: books offer a traditional means of storytelling to and for children; television exploits the widest distribution possibilities; the Web opens a range of often-interactive possibilities; licensed products provide material artifacts children use as prompts for their imagination (see Figure 3.2).

In her description of interaction on this site, Colleen details how participants' engagement is mediated through these distinct yet possibly overlapping media:

> We have sort of a model that says there's different ways that people interact with web sites, and we really want to provide sort of a sample of all of them. So [there are] things that you can passively do, like watch that cartoon; things you can actively look for like "Pet's Picks" where you can decide what station on the radio is going to download. And then things that you can vote on or that you can affect to some extent like "Prank This Cartoon," like where you can have [the characters] slide around or you know you can splat them. And then there's stuff that you can actually create yourself. And then probably the most deeply interactive is the community one-to-one interaction between fans . . . And so one thing that we are trying to do is try to provide some kind of activity for each kind of person.
>
> (2006)

*Figure 3.2* "Properties" page, depicting various ways media encourage access to and participation with *Edgar & Ellen*

Though a person's participation in some spaces will likely shape how they interact in other spaces, Colleen constructs a continuum of participation—from watching existing shows to manipulating existing characters to engaging other fans in an unscripted space. This continuum echoes many of the typical patterns of Web 2.0 participation structures that Henry Jenkins noted. For instance, Star Farm constructs low barriers for engagement, allowing fans to play games or watch videos of episodes. Star Farm cultivates the belief that children's contributions matter; users' contributions do, in fact, shape *Edgar & Ellen*. Star Farm recognizes, however, that not everyone has to contribute content, though they can when they are ready. In brief, this site allows people to participate when, and in whatever ways, they are comfortable.

Such participation is important to Colleen because, she implies, people's creativity is related to their engagement, whether that engagement develops the *Edgar & Ellen* storyline or helps participants develop new skills (e.g. create a movie) or make new friends. Across these reasons and along this engagement continuum, people modify/re-tool given community resources in ways that encourage creativity to flourish. Such creativity is fostered in dense media ecologies that are supported by a range of sponsors.

## Sponsors of creativity

Recognizing that traditional sponsors of children's education, such as teachers and librarians, are still powerful influences on children's new digital media habits, Colleen describes how all Star Farm "properties" start with books and, consequently, the courting of traditional sponsors of literacy. This courting comes in large part from *Edgar & Ellen*'s publisher Simon & Schuster, which has robust programs in place to publicize and distribute books. The publishers target librarians involved with the International Reading Association and former teachers who act as Star Farm consultants. Simon & Schuster also works with current teachers, providing supplemental instructional resources for teaching *Edgar & Ellen*, even for pitching this series to "reluctant readers;" the short chapters and detailed pictures, according to Colleen, appeal to the "id in every kid." Furthermore, Star Farm invites teachers to shape the creation of future storylines by having their students test its site, hooking students and teachers into seeing if their suggestions were heeded. Finally, Star Farm and Simon & Schuster work with children's literacy initiatives (e.g. Open Books, Orion's Mind, Boys and Girls Clubs, etc.) to encourage self-sponsored reading of this important Star Farm property (Fahey 2009).

Although starting with good stories helps court *traditional* sponsors of children's entertainment, starting with books has a second role: ensuring the story and characters are developed enough to buy credibility with *newer* sponsors, such as television and movie producers. Having sold over 450,000 books by 2007 (Press Room n.d.), *Edgar & Ellen* books have become a vehicle for Star Farm to attract sponsors of children's participation who are versed in new media, providing additional points of access for potential Star Farm patrons. Star Farm's courting of such sponsors has been quite successful. Through partnerships with over 40 businesses in English and non-English speaking countries, in television/broadcasting (e.g. Nickelodeon), in consumer products (e.g. Mattel), or in production (e.g. Bardel Entertainment Inc.), Star Farm now broadcasts the television series of *Edgar & Ellen* in over 50 countries. Moreover, the website has online visitors from over 100 countries showing the worldwide interest in Star Farm's first product.

Using *her* whole brain (e.g. the analytical skills needed for business partnerships and the innovative skills needed to imagine novel ways of forging these partnerships), Colleen is part of a team investigating how to encourage kids to use *their* whole brains to learn and think in fresh and creative ways (e.g. developing original stories designed for a range of media). Although courting traditional and new strategic global partners who run the gamut from a librarian association to big-box superstores (see Figure 3.3) complicates how Star Farm encourages various participation opportunities, cultivating these partnerships also fosters Web 2.0 environments where consumers become producers of compelling stories in new ways.

### Gamers and sponsors: Ken and David at Kuma\War

In the spring of 2007, we shadowed Ken James and David Thompson (pseudonyms) at the offices of KumaGames, which produces *Kuma\War*. Located

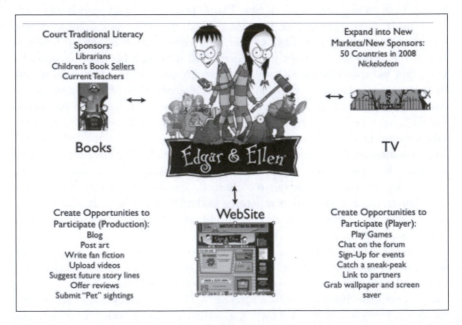

*Figure 3.3* Ways to participate in *Edgar & Ellen* via multiple media and sponsors

on the 10th floor of a New York City Park Avenue high-rise office building, KumaGames shared the floor with a hodgepodge of other, non-gaming organizations, such as the World Wildlife Fund. KumaGames' CEO and marketing director each had small individual offices with a few pictures of children and newly arrived whiteboards. Primarily, however, at least in the marketing director's office, the walls were covered by topographical maps of India, the US, the world, and various areas in Afghanistan, as well as by a large image of an animated soldier firing a weapon, likely a scene from the Afghan/Iraq simulated *Kuma\War* game.

Others in the office worked in clusters, within an open and fluid office layout that encourages the serendipitous social interaction that Malcolm Gladwell (2000) argues is critical to fostering innovation in contemporary work settings. At the KumaGames worksite, this layout included a gaming "war room," some conference rooms, a room for designing equipment, some open meeting spaces, a little cubicled office area, and a large room for designers that can best be described as a creative romper room for young men where virtual and "meat" life mix. Five young men shared this office with walls adorned by pictures of a group at a Star Trek convention (one of whom seemed to be the CEO) and a picture of a patchwork purplish cat. The whiteboard was packed with information in two columns. On the right, all tasks were crossed off except "hair cut" on the bottom, though it was unclear if this directive was for characters of a game or for one of the designers. There was a big stuffed bear on the floor, and the desk of one of the designers was cluttered with kitsch, such as a "Mr. Wonderful" toy (a male doll that, when touched, offers anti-stereotypical responses such as "I'm lost. Let's stop and ask for directions" or "No, you hold the remote"); a small brown teddy bear with "Do not disturb" written on it; and a "military babe" type action figure, which was the model for "I. Candy," a character in one of the designer's web-based games. Whether due to the spatial arrangement or the office tenor, people were constantly dropping by all of the offices (including the executives) to check in on projects, look over others' computer screens, and engage in the kind of easy back-and-forth that keeps creative ideas flowing and logistical matters on track.

In this setting, designed to encourage innovation, Ken and David discussed the central role of creativity in their work. This creativity manifested itself primarily in how producers designed thick media ecologies that offer multiple ways for players to participate. These ecologies interweave virtual and real life in ways that Ken and David believe encourage potential players to get in the game. Analysis of these ecologies, as well as the stories of the producers who shape these ecologies, highlights the influence of sponsors on participation structures, a key issue educators must also address when they attempt similar projects.

*Entertainment as the news: new models of participation*

While KumaGames has a growing number of products, its best-known game is the one that still dominates the company: *Kuma\War*. *Kuma\War* generally recreates battles that have happened in Afghanistan or Iraq, ideally within the last six months. Seeking to merge virtual and real battles, *Kuma\War* re-mixes actual and faux news coverage, as it creates a range of participation structures for gamers. This blurring of being in and out of the game pervades *Kuma\War* from its tag line, "Real War News. Real War Games," to its mission page, which describes how subscribers to *Kuma\War* can "experience *first-hand* some of the toughest fighting in the global war on terror because each mission is based on real-world events" (emphasis added).

Just as he did in real life, even after his capture and death, Saddam Hussein figures prominently in *Kuma\War*, literally in the scope of those coming to the game. Top banners depicting insurgents, neighborhood buildings that can hide insurgents, and Coalition Forces with tanks blazing could all double as faux news coverage of the War on Terror, with only the rotating image of business partners betraying the explicit corporate sponsoredness of this site.

In *Kuma\War*, the mission videos riff on CNN war coverage, picking up this network's red lettering, a similar font, and a tagline format that runs across bottom of screen. In addition, *Kuma\War* provides actual aerial photos and nestles the game within real news coverage, which contains both authentic images of US military missions and links to existing global news stories, thereby allowing players—in their real- and virtual-world identities—to gather as many facts as possible. This blurring extends to the mission video where the faux news anchor interviews real, retired military personnel to contextualize actual footage of military operations that become the basis for the game.

Toward the end of *Kuma\War*'s mission video—after players learn of the mission objectives, hear how the mission went, and gather vital reconnaissance about sites in play—the focus shifts to the game itself. There are direct instructions about game goals and set-up options from Jak, a late twenties-ish, attractive female in a tight but casual t-shirt, who presents herself as a designer of the game (though when we were at *Kuma\War*, there was not a single female employee on permanent staff). Jak is a knowledgeable guide, giving enough information quickly so that regular players know what to do and providing clues so newcomers can pick up tips that may help them live a bit longer. For example, Jak often voices over images from the game, pointing out where people need to be careful, how they can heal themselves, and what their objectives should be.

*Kuma\War*'s intertwining of real-world and virtual information creates architectures of participation that encourage participants to anticipate their virtual game play even when out of the game, a move, according to James Paul Gee (2003), that is common in video games. According to Gee, blurring virtual and real worlds and identities happens when players manage their multiple identities: a virtual identity is "one's identity as a virtual character" in the world of the video game (54); a real-world identity is one's identity as a "nonvirtual person playing a computer game" (55); and a projective identity is the "interface between—the interactions between—the real world person and the virtual character" (56). Projective identities enable players to imagine their real-world identity as their virtual identity.

Adding Gee to our theoretical framework, we argue that to encourage players to "own" their projective identities, designers develop architectures that help players imagine themselves in the space between the potential of their virtual identity and the limits of their real-world identities. As gamers become legitimate participants in these communities by taking up the community's desired actions, values, and norms, players are enticed to work hard and achieve meaningful success within these communities. Through such participation, according to Gee, gamers can learn new ways of thinking/being in the world. And, while certainly not a given, these new ways of seeing and being that a game provides can encourage gamers to take new, even innovative orientations toward ways of being and knowing in the real world, as *Kuma\War* illustrates here and as Sarah Robbins describes more fully below.

### Technological affordances and participation

The projective identities of *Kuma\War* are being built, in part, through the technological affordances of the game, and producers use these affordances to remediate how people interact with technology. In fact, KumaGames's tag line, "TV for people raised on Games," provokes a rethinking of what people raised on games expect and want from their engagement with all media. The image of gaming evoked in KumaGames's older version of its logo depicts a retro *Space Invaders*-style image that has an open square as its belly, indicating that television is being subsumed/consumed by the interactions of video games. This image of gaming then is geared for not only the 97% of teens who have played video games (Lenhart et al. 2008), but also the forty-somethings who played *Space Invaders* in the 1970s and 1980s.

KumaGames remediates people's understanding by offering a range of new and traditional participation structures through the media. In a controversial claim, Ken argues that, as people have moved from listening to radio, to watching television, to engaging with online games, media has facilitated more active participation. While players can participate in the *Kuma\War* activities in isolation, the jargon on KumaGames's splash page makes clear KumaGames is shooting for interactivity: "Nearly 100 playable missions bring our soldiers' heroic stories to life, and you can get them all right now, for free. Stop watching the news and get in the game!" (*Kuma\War* splash page 2008).

One way this interactivity works is when games remake the experience of watching television so that watching itself becomes interactive. For example, people can watch The History Channel in anticipation of impending games on *Kuma\War*, taking notes individually or emailing team players about how they could adapt information from The History Channel episode for their *Kuma\War* game playing. A second form of interactivity is found while playing the game. For many, the game constitutes an environment that encourages people to engage with each other, and players can "get in the game" in a variety of ways: as an individual playing alone; with a group of players unknown to each other beforehand; in clans, where regular groups meet to play the game in what become familiar ways. In all of the multiplayer participation possibilities, interactivity is foregrounded: "You may all be enemies on the playing field, but nowhere else is the chat as friendly and entertaining as it is in a RedonBlue [match up between two or more teams] session;" "Working as one unstoppable force is how it's done in the real-world operations, and scores of multiplayers like to replicate the missions cooperatively" (Multiplayer introduction n.d.).

Players take up these participant roles in a variety of ways, but one thing that designers hope unites these possibilities is a sense of being a member of a community. This community is built not only by geographically dispersed people coming together to play games every week, much like the long-lost bowlers Robert Putnam (2000) describes in *Bowling Alone*, but also in less obvious, face-to-face ways. Comparing *Kuma\War* to things like television sitcoms and baseball, Ken argues that *Kuma\War* can build community due to the social aspects of people sitting around the proverbial water cooler re-hashing the serial KumaGame "episodes." In fact, Ken believes that these discussions around *Kuma\War*'s serialization—a new "episode" (war game) each Tuesday to Friday night—contradict the stereotypical depiction of video games as solitary and anti-social. Like Colleen Fahey who finds community building to be the most interactive and highest point on a participation continuum for children at Star Farm (implying this participation is central to children becoming fearlessly creative), the CEO at KumaGames also emphasizes participating in community as a social good, though this KumaGames executive is more overt in linking community engagement with keeping eyeballs, and therefore revenue, on the site. This highly social aspect of gaming, Ken believes, is fostered through serial, interactive programs and foretells future trends. Drawing together players' virtual and real-world identities, these future trends combine interpersonal desires for connection with gaming's ability to cash in on fostering these connections.

### Complications of sponsorship

Even though simulated fighting of insurgents is a common video game trope, *Kuma\War* founders feared receiving bad press that made them out to be "profiteers" of the war. Both Ken and David oppose this view and want to avoid any such associations with their fledgling three-year-old company. Arguing that folks at Halliburton are profiteering on the war, not them, David goes on to say that if people accept that war games are a viable activity, then they can't be upset with KumaGames. Even so, this fear shaped how overtly Ken and David talked about their two primary sponsors: the US military and The History Channel.

When describing their direct and indirect relationships with the US military, Ken and David often seemed defensive. Generally, they described their relationship with this sponsor within a framework of service. As David argues, this game serves civilians by providing a perspective and a simulated experience of being in these battles: "Armed with identical weapons in a realistic re-creation of various locations, you'll experience some of [the] fiercest engagements in the most hostile territories in the world" (Splash page 2008).

More significant to their argument about KumaGames's service, Ken claims that *Kuma\War* benefits and is valued by active military personnel. For the upper levels of the military, *Kuma\War* provides a sympathetic portrayal of an often unpopular war. To facilitate this representation, senior military officials comprise an advisory board that offers *Kuma\War* designers specific suggestions to make *Kuma\War* games more accurate from the military's perspective. As advertised on *Kuma\War*'s splash page, "A vast database of intelligence accompanies *Kuma\War* online games; satellite photos, political context, event details and the weaponry, tactics and forces involved. You'll also get exclusive video news shows and insight from a decorated team of military veterans" (n.d.).

For ground soldiers, *Kuma\War* presents battles in a more controlled and perhaps favorable way, enabling soldiers to relive painful experiences from a safe distance. For example, on *Kuma\War*'s website, one "Quotes from Players in the Trenches" states, "This game actually makes me flash back and think about the war and the aftermath . . . But that's not necessarily bad. Being that I will be going back to Iraq for a 3rd tour, I'll say that it's much better fighting from my PC behind a desk then [sic] actually slinging lead at each other" (Splash page 2008). Attending to active duty military personnel has been significant in *Kuma\War*'s history. In fact, David reported that when *Kuma\War* was subscription-based, as much as 20–25% of participants were in the military. And, while KumaGames is now ad-based which makes accurate statistics about users no longer possible, Ken and David relay that significant numbers of military personnel still email regularly to report on how they want KumaGames to represent their military experiences.

Similarly, Ken and David believe the benefits of *Kuma\War* for military extend beyond active duty to those who have returned. Like the soldier above who was about to face his third deployment, some returning soldiers, according to Ken, play the game to lessen the trauma of their experience. Although he acknowledges he lacks hard evidence, Ken likened the opportunities *Kuma\War* provides to returning veterans to the opportunities afforded to 9/11 fire fighters in their repeated computer simulations of the events of that day—as a way to help them work through their distress. This argument carried strong emotional resonances in New York City, where, even at the time of our 2006 interview, the memories of the Twin Towers's collapse still powerfully resonated.

Although David and Ken were discreet, even guarded, about their relationship with the US military, they were overt about their relationship with another pivotal sponsor of KumaGames: The History Channel. For this partnership,

*Kuma\War* make three interactive games per season based on battles featured in a History Channel episode. At the end of the episode, The History Channel announces that viewers who would like to learn more can go to KumaWar.com and relive the battle by playing the games. Despite the facts that The History Channel has a slightly older demographic and that KumaGames had never previously run games on World War II or Vietnam (the episodes agreed upon for the first collaboration), this cross-advertising provides great press for both companies; it helps The History Channel move to a new medium and introduces gaming in general, and KumaGames in particular, to a vast audience. This introduction, however, is not without complications, as we'll discuss below.

The History Channel's sponsorship is part of KumaGames's CEO's goal of locating *Kuma\War* within a rich media ecology. In addition to The History Channel, KumaGames has a MySpace account for "I. Candy," the highly sexualized and only female character in the game *Dino-Hunters*. On MySpace, I. Candy has a blog and numerous "friends," who, we would guess, are more technologically proficient than most members of The History Channel audience. Moreover, KumaGames is exploring how to pitch tie-ins to popular television shows. Beyond the explicit connections with various media, the *Kuma\War* designers draw the game into other media ecologies when the designers watch movies (e.g. *Ice Age*) to capture movements and even code for KumaGame backgrounds. Similarly, designers model their own splash pages on popular websites (e.g. The Cartoon Network) that attempt to manage a similar design of content options, encouraging navigation strategies that "make it as easy as possible to hit a button" (*Kuma\War* game designer 2006) and either stay on this site or go to sponsors' sites, thus reinforcing the tight links within the *Kuma\War* ecology.

Within this far-reaching ecology, Ken and David saw sponsorships with both the US military and The History Channel as a win-win. With the military, *Kuma\War* receives more detailed military information that strengthens the accuracy of the game and the military receives good press for civilians, encouragement from and for active (and future) troops, and an opportunity for what Ken believes is a sort of healing for returning veterans. With The History Channel, *Kuma\War* attracts large audiences—perhaps the greatest resource that the fledgling KumaGames needed—and The History Channel has developed a contemporary, cross-platform collaboration. Yet, while these sponsorships offer benefits *Kuma\War* values, they also come with tacit and explicit expectations—generally positive portrayal of military actions; the need to alter *Kuma\War*'s primary focus on battles in Iraq and Afghanistan to include battles from World War II and Vietnam, etc.—that highlight the invisible influence sponsors exert on the entities involved. Most notably, *Kuma\War*'s sponsors shape the complex architectures of participation that *Kuma\War* designers create to help players mediate their virtual, projective, and real-world identities. In short, the expectations of *Kuma\War*'s sponsors shape the participation structures and, therefore, the types of creativity encouraged in these sites.

*Death and rebirth of History Channel watchers: a teaching moment of a real kind*

As educators, we can learn quite a lot about the structures needed to encourage new learning possibilities, if we examine the "teaching moments" that producers of *Kuma\War* face on a regular basis. For example, when *Kuma\War* partnered with The History Channel, they ran into fundamental problems. As History Channel patrons visited *Kuma\War*, they brought much-coveted "eyeballs" that could raise *Kuma\War*'s profile, patronage, and, therefore, bottom line, but these potential gamers also brought a lack of understanding about gaming. Coming to *Kuma\War* to experience their fascination with battles of years past in a new way, these "newbies" were overloaded with stimuli—rich visuals, streaming video, and aural commands that these gaming novices generally did not grasp—as they struggled to participate in simulated war activities. Then, the virtual identities of these inexperienced game players frequently died. Immediately and repeatedly. To keep new gamers' "eyeballs," *Kuma\War* needed to provide intensely scaffolded instructions non-gamers could understand. And yet, in *Kuma\War*'s pursuit to court and keep this new market, producers of *Kuma\War* faced the danger of alienating their base of active gamers by providing too much didactic help or slow game play. How could KumaGames employ conventionalized strategies that gamers would know (e.g. how to find a medical kit to repair oneself and therefore stay alive and keep fighting) when new players did not know the conventions? In short, how could the producers challenge and entice a range of participants at different levels to learn what they need to progress to the next level?

Although the producers at *Kuma\War* framed these questions as an issue of keeping potential market share, we frame this dilemma within the context educators face daily, while recognizing that *Kuma\War* has some significant advantages over educators. For example, like participants at Star Farm and, as we'll see in the next section, on *Second Life*, *Kuma\War* participants come voluntarily and are invested in learning. Moreover, *Kuma\War* has the real advantage in its immediate feedback loop. When *Kuma\War* does a good job, designers can watch the games and note where it is working. When *Kuma\War* has not provided enough information for the new gamers to succeed, they can watch gamers logout or, even more disconcerting, see their help lines swamped with angry, virtually-dead gamers.

Despite these advantages, *Kuma\War* has much to teach educators. At KumaGames, designers create new games/learning environments by building on familiar media tropes when creating interfaces, such as embedding an element of *Ice Age* into some backdrop for a game or drawing on common templates (e.g. The Cartoon Network) for interaction. Moreover, successful learning at *Kuma\War* relies on motivated audiences finding multiple, varied paths into participating in a supportive community that both challenges veteran players and legitimates the influence of new players. As *Kuma\War* illustrates, it is both the human community and the virtual architecture that provide a structured environment rich with scaffolded help and an expert "on call" for immediate guidance in case things go awry. This is a powerful design for learning.

### Creativity in Web 2.0 Worlds:
### Sarah "Intellagirl" Robbins's Architectures of Participation

Mary P. met Sarah Robbins—author, academic, and media consultant, whose quotation opens this chapter—the year before her interview and was impressed by Sarah's contagious curiosity about how to design learning environments that foster creativity and innovation. For Sarah, this design cannot be separated from the spaces that encourage such creative activity. These environments, or what Sarah calls "architectures of participation," combine Henry Jenkins's ideas of the Web 2.0 world's participatory culture with the legitimate participation that Lave and Wenger found essential for learning in a range of face-to-face, out of school contexts. When a friend mentioned Sarah had just co-authored *Second Life for Dummies* (2008), we thought she would be perfect for this study.

Born in 1975, just three years before *Space Invaders*' Japanese debut, Sarah claims that computers have always been a part of her life. Like painting and knitting, computer programming has allowed her to express her creativity since grammar school. According to Sarah, learning to use computers had an added benefit: "I could do something that other people couldn't do" (2008). This distinction heightened Sarah's desire to be an early adopter, a practice that helped her land her first job at Que, later part of Pearson Publishing. As the developmental editor for the *Complete Idiot's Guides*, Sarah became involved in online communities that helped her learn the newest trends and build a community of support.

Three years into her job, Sarah became pregnant with triplets and had to go on bed rest. As they had when she went away to college, computers once again provided her with a way to deal with change and isolation; this time, she played lots of games and became a guild leader in *Star Wars Galaxy*. In the six years since her children were born, Sarah has kept up her online gaming, furthering her participation in a rich media ecology:

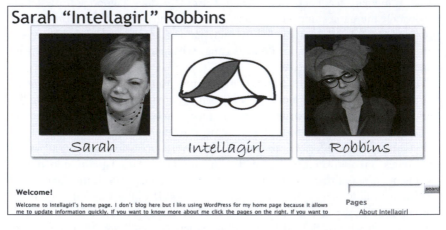

*Figure 3.4* Top of Sarah Robbins's splash page

I am the editor in several blogs, I have my own blog, I have my own website. I create content in *Second Life* on a pretty regular basis. I do some web design. I twitter all of the time. And all of those forms meet a different need for communication; they reach different people in different ways for different purposes.

(2008)

As a self-described highly social person, Sarah self-consciously complicates the pervasive arguments that claim communication technologies such as IM, cell phones, and the internet promote bee-like exchanges that fail to foster critical, thoughtful discourse, and therefore relationships (cf. Olds and Schwartz 2009). Contrary to this representation, Sarah is highly reflective and discerning about how she uses communication technologies to meet a variety of connection possibilities.

Among our many interviewees, Sarah is unusually articulate about how the structures of online environments construct participation, and she attributes this clarity to her graduate work in rhetorical studies. In describing her work, Sarah claims, "I am rhetorical about everything, so I am thinking, who is this space for and what is the intended action that we want? How do we want people to behave in this space? And what's going to keep them coming back?" (2008). Very comfortably, Sarah uses classical rhetorical frameworks to help her make sense of contemporary, digitally mediated possibilities for persuading an audience to take action. To foster this action, Sarah focuses on architectures of participation that encourage connection and communication in both her personal and professional work: her PhD research is on how communication mechanics in virtual environments motivate people to participate in certain ways; her volunteer work with a new marketing company seeks to create local social networks into a virtual "Smaller Indiana;" and her paid positions include being a blogger for hire and a consultant to universities and businesses on *Second Life*. In all of these settings, Sarah critically analyzes how to tap the affordances of particular communication technologies in order to encourage participation structures that motivate her audience to act.

*Participation structures in Web 2.0*

Involvement in Web 2.0 requires that the designers of digital spaces foster participation structures that move a user from passive reading/watching to action. This change from seeing the Web as a dumping ground for information (a negative take on Web 1.0) to a space that calls people to connect through social networking indicates the shift to a Web 2.0 mentality. In her interview, Sarah explains her Web 2.0 participation emphasis:

It used to be that you valued something, some form of media, by how many people looked at it. "We've got a tenth of the share in our time slot for our TV show and that's not enough so we want more viewers."

And now it's much more specific than that. It's not [about attracting] a lot of people; it's [about attracting] the right people. I don't care that 1,000 people hit the *Second Life* [SLED] blog a day. *What I care is about whether I can get them to comment and whether I can get them to follow the links to other resources.* Because I can get lots of traffic, but we need meaningful traffic. It's just a different metric of success . . . How do we know that we were successful? What do we want people to do? *What action do we want them to take?* And, for my personal blog, it's "hey—contact me and ask me to publish something or contact me and offer to pay me to come do a talk." For the SLED blog it's very different. It's getting people to want to contribute to the blog or get them to comment on a blog post and start a discussion that will encourage other people to continue to talk. So it's kind of a snowball effect that you really want. *It's a different strategy for content creation.*

(2008, emphasis added)

As Sarah's words suggests, the goal of web generation is shifting from a model based on the transmission of information (i.e. Web 1.0), where the goal was to get someone's attention, to a model based on fostering someone's participation (Web 2.0). As people create online spaces, they construct architectures that encourage certain types of participation that are desired in this environment (e.g. to post blog) or as a result of this environment (e.g. hire Sarah as a consultant).

To get people to participate, Sarah thinks and writes explicitly about architectures of participation (Web 2.0 for Business n.d.), which require producers to develop spaces that encourage certain rules of interaction. For Sarah, these interactions seek to create opportunities to be challenged, creative, and successful; opportunities to participate in and design new environments; and opportunities to play. Central to all of these opportunities is fostering participants' motivation to be in these spaces. For example, when discussing her creation of two islands for the Alumni Relations department of a large public university, Sarah describes how she moves from the university's goal of having folks come back to the motives users might have for taking up this goal:

Going from their goals and what they wanted—which is a place that people want to come back to and want to spend time in—okay, what kind of spaces do people do that in in the real world? And how can we do that in a way that will make it worth their time to go online, to learn this new piece of software? What's going to be the payoff, what's going to make it worth it?

(2008)

For Sarah, spaces elicit actions based on or by shaping participants' motives, and because people's motives vary, producers need to provide multiple ways into an online environment.

### *Motivation in online spaces*

Sarah most explicitly describes the multiple ways people may be motivated to participate when referring to a website for children, which Sarah's own children use: ePets.

According to Sarah, children find many ways into online games, often in relation to their motivation for learning. For example, Sarah narrates the way her three six-year-old children play with their e-pet, a virtual animal:

> Keagan likes to play games and earn coins. She's very motivated by finishing things. She wants to accomplish stuff and get a reward, so she'll sit down for twenty minutes and play games and earn coins. And then Morgan will sit down and she will spend all of the coins for clothing for the dog. Which makes Keagan mad and Keagan has to earn more coins. Alexander just wants to stand over their shoulder and say, "oh, click that, click that." . . .
>
> Keagan, she wants to finish things and get a reward for it. She wants to say, "look at how many coins I won. Look, I did it. And I beat that other dog in the race." And that to her is successful. And for Morgan, it's successful to take the dog to the beauty parlor. And give it a bath and change what color it is.

(2008)

*Figure 3.5* My ePets splash page

65

Sarah believes that successful architectures of participation encourage a variety of motivations in online gaming. One thing these diverse motivations share is an opportunity to be challenged, creative, and successful.

An additional shared motive is the possibility to participate in and create new environments, even if the possibilities afforded by online architectures of participation are tempered by the constraints of the community norms and the media ecologies that shape participation in each site. For all new media, one of these constraints is a user's imagination when it comes to participating on a site. Often, people are blinded to new possibilities by what has come before. People map past applications onto new possibilities because that is what they know. Sarah picks up Sarah Sloane's (1999) description of this problem, media haunting, in her own work:

> There is an article in [*Passions and Pedagogies*] called the "The Haunting Story of J" [about] media haunting [where] you use a new media like you used the media that came before it. You use a word processor like you used a typewriter until you get used to it and then you start to play with the new features . . . I think *Second Life* is a version, is a new, is like "real world 2.0." You know? People come in and their initial thing is to create an avatar that looks just like them and then they start to experiment with, well, "why do I have to be white? Why can't I be green? Green, that'll be cool." And they start to experiment and play. And the building in the spaces is about the same . . . So universities would come and they would rebuild their campus to the detail and then nobody would come; nobody would hang out there. *And so as people get used to what the medium can create and what the affordances are, they get more creative.* So now we see instructors who teach dressed up as a dragon because why not? There is nothing to stop you from being a dragon when you teach . . . *And the mechanics create the culture. What you can do sort of starts to dictate what you should or shouldn't do.* It's really interesting to see those kinds of rules develop.
>
> (2008; emphasis added)

Whether with individual avatars or university *Second Life* islands, new producers often use the affordances of new media to do familiar things in not-so-different ways. But as comfort with digitally mediated environments grows, possibilities grow as well. Producers take the readily available tools to explore alternatives in ways that encourage new, and often creative, ways of thinking. In *Second Life*, for example, the tools encourage people to participate in and design new environments. Digital technologies open worlds that are initially foreign but this foreignness becomes inviting; "what is here?" becomes "what can be here?" To analyze the existing conditions and to imagine future possibilities of these conditions, people in online environments encounter a "mechanics of culture" that, ideally, elicits whole brain creativity.

Similar to Colleen, Ken, and David, Sarah finds that what unites many of the spaces is a sense of play, of having imaginative experiences people can't get in the real world. For Sarah, play is about creative problem solving, both for producers keeping people's attention and for users feeling compelled to engage in a certain way. One way play does this is by garnering attention and building a desire for people to return. In today's attention economy (cf. Lankshear and Knobel 2001) where information is everywhere, distracting and overwhelming, Sarah knows she is competing with many channels that vie for people's consideration. She describes this most clearly when talking about her university classes that use *Second Life*:

> So when I'm teaching students *Second Life* I have to know that [students] could be SMSing on their phones, they could have music playing, they've got video from YouTube, and all kinds of other stuff. Twitter and everything else. And so, how can I compete? How can I make my message the one that they tune into the most? That they want to listen to at that point. Even in the face-to-face classroom we're competing with those things and certainly when we're talking about marketing and talking about consumers. They've got so many different choices and so many different voices talking to them all at once. So how do you not get filtered out?
>
> (2008)

Sarah believes playful design is one thing that can help to keep her from getting filtered out. Whether planning a lesson for her teaching or inviting people to develop online resources for small businesses in Indiana, Sarah responds to her users' desires, in part, by considering how play can tap the affordances of online spaces to keep people invested in her spaces.

As Sarah makes clear, play is central to the media-rich worlds of our multitasking students. In many video games such as those at *Edgar & Ellen* and *Kuma\ War*, play allows people to participate in new worlds in embodied, situated ways that foster learning opportunities seldom realized in schools (cf. Gee 2003; Shaffer et al. 2005). And yet, educators often prefer the idea of "rigor" to that of "play," fearing that play may be a distraction from educational goals. Some fear is legitimate, yet not all of it. For Colleen, Ken, David, and Sarah, play forges communities that work together. This play can unite people, start discussions, and encourage individuals to pursue community inflected goals. Thus, through creating participation structures that encourage certain kinds of play, designers can embed the outcomes that educators desire with rigor as part of the process.

Evoking her understandings of Web 2.0's possibility to enact a prosumer education (e.g. users shaping technologies; less hierarchical content generation, etc.),[4] Sarah offers many suggestions about how to encourage this play. In particular, Sarah seeks to capitalize on contemporary means of communication and learning—means that many of our students already know—explaining her adoption of prosumer education in a fuller version of the quotation excerpted at the opening of this chapter:

> I definitely think there needs to be an emphasis on learners creating their own content. The whole Web 2.0 movement and the prosumer movement put the means of production in the hands of everybody.
>
> It used to be that it was the people who could afford the software and afford a computer that could do it, were the ones who created content. And now, everyone can do it; it is a matter of quality rather than the facility.
>
> So, to use *Second Life* for example, there is no reason why an instructor or an educational technologist should build an island for a class. Students should do it because they can. They should create the space that they most want to learn in and they should create their own learning tools . . . So definitely [I support] that idea of prosumer education, of the instructor stepping aside and acting more as a travel guide and letting the students lead the way. And the kinds of things the traditional age student now, the kinds of things that they do for fun, the forms of media that they create voluntarily on their own time for fun. There is no reason why those forms shouldn't take prime center seat in the classroom, as far as I am concerned. If we know now that teenage girls are producing so much content online and yet we don't see them producing that much more in the classroom, why? If we carry those kinds of philosophies that we are seeing from the technology culture into the classroom I think we are going to see really big developments.
>
> (2008)

When Sarah argues that teachers should step aside, she is not abdicating the responsibility of the teacher's role. Teachers must accept the responsibility of creating an environment and scaffolded activities that encourage the learning outcomes they desire. And yet, Sarah argues that teachers need to do this in a way that allows students to be active learners, even leaders and/or producers in that learning. In the 21st-century context of what seems a more traditional Deweyian precept, Sarah lauds the possibilities through which digital technologies enable all students to become producers. In their own productions, students are more engaged—they are designing spaces for future actions, investigating genuine questions where teachers and students work together in new ways, and examining how their extra-curricular learning can be brought into the classroom as an advantage in building connections within and outside of school. Such digitally mediated learning is the present and future of education, not just because these environments are common to our students, but because these environments provide opportunities for effective pedagogy within contemporary classrooms.

## Conclusion

If we want to encourage learning with communities of creative and engaged participants, then we need to design environments that encourage creative and engaged ways of acting and thinking.[5] These environments should be thought of as architectures of participation that provide legitimate sites of learning where people can meaningfully contribute, receive constructive feedback, and shape the community—often as producers who are ratified, valued members of their community. A pedagogy based on this premise requires people not just to acquire content, but also to cultivate a disposition toward creative problem-solving, a project that calls people to use the analytic and creative sides of their whole brain. To pursue such a goal, educators can learn several lessons from the digital media producers we studied.

One such lesson calls for attention to structures; educators need to build structures that foster creativity and innovation, goals rampant across recent educational reports (cf. Bearne et al. 2004; US Department of Education 2006). Whereas some educators and institutions are essential to the creativity that underscores community innovation, such as when universities host business incubators and start entrepreneurial programs that seek creative ways to approach fleeting opportunities and trenchant problems (cf. Knievel and Sheridan-Rabideau 2009), too often schools not only fail to build the structures that facilitate creativity, but they often disregard out-of-school sites of creativity and innovation that students bring to the classroom. As Joan A. Rhodes and Valerie J. Robnolt (2009) note:

> Schooling continues to be based on paper-based literacy instead of practices that allow students to explore and utilize the multimodal, nonlinear literacies available in digital environments. Digital natives (Prensky, 2001) arriving in today's classrooms are working in an environment that does not match their learning needs and/or the changes in the way their minds process information.
>
> (158)

Rhodes and Robnolt continue that, because educators neither recognize nor exploit the possibilities of these digital environments, students are becoming "less engaged" in this "old-style instruction" and "enraged" with teachers who are not changing their curricula to meet these students' needs (158).

The consequence of teachers being unresponsive to today's changing conditions is that we risk becoming irrelevant to students who find "old-style instruction" only marginally helpful as they tackle 21st-century challenges. By contrast, the producers we interviewed worked hard to be responsive, encouraging users to be active generators of shared knowledge (Colleen), innovating on traditional ways to support new and continuing learners (Ken and David), figuring ways to keep students "tuned in" to their classes (Sarah), in part by having users be producers of the learning environments they want to inhabit. These strategies—promoting creative and analytical skills; designing multiple and varied ways into a site, and then offering the support and success for users to continue; developing environments where people can engage as legitimate participants in communities—are the foundation to good pedagogy. The challenge for educators is how to integrate these participation structures in our classrooms.

A second lesson focuses on using contemporary tools to encourage people to think in new and creative ways. In particular, with the new tools afforded by digital media people can push on the known or expected, thus opening up new possibilities even with what seem like staid static practices. Colleen, for instance, notes how many kids today are already engaging in creative uses of traditional practices when they are in dense media ecologies.

> Today's digital kids are not consuming media the way they used to, sort of one at a time. [Instead] you could be watching television on the website, you could be reading a book and going to Google to find out more about some aspect of the book or what a word means. You could have an iPod on while you're doing your computer.
>
> (2007)

Colleen believes that successful engagement with youth today requires understanding how people operate within and across media ecologies that change our experience of everyday practices, in this case reading, writing, and listening. When seemingly agreed upon, semi-static practices are located in new architectures, people participate in reading, writing, and listening practices in very different ways. These changes mean that those "schooled" in different communities and participation structures experience school-valued practices (e.g. reading, composing) differently. In short, new tools elicit new practices, which call educators to rethink how to reach and teach our students.

A third lesson concerns sponsors; when educators or producers design participation structures that invite people to explore opportunities for creative engagement via new tools, they must negotiate how old and new sponsors shape this invitation to participate.

There are several key sponsors of learning. Historically, the primary category of sponsorship has been from schools, and yet the producers we studied are mixed in their assessment of this sponsorship. In the positive camp, Colleen details how Star Farm and its distributors heavily court former and present librarians and teachers. Sarah Robbins is also invested in school-based sponsors, perhaps because she is completing her PhD with hopes of teaching in a university setting. Even with this positioning, however, Sarah tempers her endorsement of educational sponsorship, calling on teachers to meet contemporary conditions with new tools and mindsets.

Other producers in business, the community, and the academy are more skeptical of the effectiveness of schools. These producers argue that educators are not teaching our students how to develop creative mindsets, nor are they designing environments and practices to encourage creative thinking (cf. Carrington 2008; Gee 2003; Shaffer et al. 2005; Yancey 2008). At KumaGames, young game designers strongly articulated this position, noting a profound disconnect between their recent years of schooling and what they do now. Like many of the producers we interviewed, these *Kuma\War* designers argue that students would learn better if academics followed the freedom of inquiry, collaboration, and peer-creation of gaming models.

A second key category of educational sponsorship is the marketplace. Our interviews make clear there is much educators can learn from prosumer tenets, such as how creative dispositions are fostered in structurally open learning environments, with peer-generated knowledge making, and through the push for students to be producers. We support these claims even as we foreground that classrooms have their own constraints and models that do not match perfectly with marketplace structures. Consequently, despite the real promise of marketplace sponsors, we caution against wholesale adoption of the contemporary euphoric discourses swirling around how markets define prosumer education—the complicated relationships between education, creativity, and consumerism need to be carefully examined (cf. Jenkins et al. 2007; Scanlon and Buckingham 2004).

These three lessons highlight that although learning is highly situated—and these situations require local, specific enactments—our interviewees share a commitment to fostering a creative, problem-solving disposition. Such a disposition is advanced through architectures of participation that call people to become creative members of communities that, in these cases, use 21st-century tools to experiment and innovate.

In the next chapter, we explore these ideas further as we examine how specific producers materialize their creative innovations as they spin their ideas.

# 4

# THE ART OF SPIN

Through a range of modes (visual, audio, written, and so on) producers spin products that users "consume." Consumers then redesign, both directly and indirectly, the original text, creating new remixed products that others consume and remix. These are the texts that pervade our world. On a daily basis, *The New York Times* and other leading newspapers spotlight a freshly minted spin-product. Spin takes an idea and materializes it through strategic choice of modes. As just one example, on the front page of *The New York Times*, September 20, 2009, the technology section introduces four spin products:

> A start-up in Colorado has a new twist on print publishing. It lets read-ers pick which articles they want in their magazine and print it them-selves . . . Readers can print a copy of the magazine or view it online or on a mobile device.
>
> (Miller 2009)

> The star video game developer behind *Age of Empires* has turned his gaming talents to something new: teaching children languages. Wiz World Online, developed by 8D World, a start-up based in Shanghai, China, and Wodburn, Mass., was built by Rick Goodman, who devel-oped the popular games *Age of Empires* and *Empire Earth*. Instead of re-enacting historical battles, he is having Chinese children learn English in a virtual world.
>
> (Miller 2009)

> The Internet Corporation for Assigned Names and Numbers, the group charged with assigning the domain names used by Web sites, is about to let anyone start a top-level domain—the part of an Internet address to the right of the period. It says this plan will let entrepreneurs sell specialty addresses to people and companies interested in certain areas, like .shoes or .movies.
>
> (Miller 2009)

> Some internet bad guys are exploiting interest in the new Harry Potter movie to further their devious plot to make mischief online. Their target is people who can be enticed to watch an illegal copy of "Harry Potter and the Half-Blood Prince" on the Web.
>
> (Miller 2009)

A brief survey of a leading newspaper is enough to indicate an exploding industry of remixed products that readers and users take up and remix themselves. Digital environments give users greater access and modal affordances to remix ideas. Contemporary spin works on digital systems of knowledge and the affordances of animation, visuals, sound, etc. For example, *The New York Times* online edition, nytimes.com, provides frequent reminders about the nytimes.com/bits blog, which is updated every day. This is a different experience from flipping pages while sitting in a chair reading *The New York Times*. Everything sold on the market needs a digital face to succeed. From newspapers, to life coaching, to clothing lines, digital media cast an image, an impression for users to assess. Digital media and what it exudes has so much to do with how we take it up. If digital media is well designed, inviting, a place where you want to go and buy products, then the spin has succeeded.

During the democratic race for nomination, digital media provided a means to differentiate between Hilary Clinton and Barack Obama. Seen as a PC platform, Clinton exuded more of a conservative, business-minded ethic tied to PC users and PC interface. Seen as a Mac platform, Obama exuded more of a progressive, edgy stance tied to Mac users and Mac interface. Newspapers and news broadcasters have relative carte blanche with modal choice and use modal choice as a way to spin a text/product. Spin is not reserved to news forums in that digital media is a first line of analysis in general, and spin mediates what gets understood about all types of products.

Spinning is the process of fleshing out a story for a text. Spin frames an interpretation in a manner similar to Erving Goffman's notion of "frame space" (Goffman 1981). In *Forms of Talk*, Goffman talks about the concept of "frame space" as, "in brief, when the individual speaks, he avails himself of certain options and forgoes others" and in so doing occupies a "frame space" (1981: 230). Despite what seems like a neat, linear process, spinning a story can be messy and uncertain. Goffman (1981) considers how speakers' uses of contextual cues provide frames for listeners. He uses the term "frame" as a way to understand and explain talk-in-interaction. Framing and reframing are ways of influencing an interpretation and reinterpretation of interactional content. Designing a text or product means framing the idea through modes that can be remixed or redesigned from previous texts or designed from scratch. The movement from a controlling idea to a text spins a story, but, along the way, there are events, people, and other texts that make the process more random and idiosyncratic.

As an idiosyncratic process, to spin a product requires a person and a motivating factor. Producers and design teams move ideas to a story, encountering and engaging with structures, limitations, and constraints throughout production. Although previously carrying a negative connotation, "spindoctors" have expertise in identifying a convincing way of composing an idea in multiple modes. Being a spindoctor is a disposition common to our participant producers. Revisiting some of our producers in Table 4.1 reveals a pattern in the ways producers use spin to weave a story through designs and redesigns. From a reading series to digital media, each producer in Table 4.1 shares a capacity for framing, remixing, constructing architectures of participation, and embedding sponsors into texts.

Embedded, articulated and materialized in multiple ways, each of these producers puts a unique spin on texts/products that they design. The sampling of participants in Table 4.1 gives a brief look at spin that is extended in three focal case studies in the next section.

"Spin" is a 21st-century literacy practice. It is a key disposition for making meaning with texts. Fanzines, iPods, and Youtube have been around in some guise for ages, but the 21st-century rendition of them offers a different form and function. Fanzines were previously in paper form, yet still carried the same purpose as the online version as articles about fandom. Similarly, an iPod is a distant relative of a predecessor, a Walkman. Finally, Youtube resembles abridged versions of filmic narratives such as trailers at the beginning of movies. The point is, in spinning known technologies to be more and do more for users, we have fulfilled the life that Marshall McLuhan predicted when he wrote, "the

*Table 4.1* Sampling of spindoctors

| Spindoctor/s | Spun design |
| --- | --- |
| Warren Beavis | Designs a safe, nurturing, inviting digital environment for victims of domestic violence. |
| Kim Cartesh | Remixes the *Family Guy* television show into digital environment mediating applications with a network capacity (architectures of participation) with sponsors such as Burger King. |
| José Garcia | Design of *Dora the Explorer* emerged from a word 'computerdora' and interface and televisual text that captures bilingualism, problem-solving, venturing out into the community. |
| Robert Hammer and Alan Katsky | Design reading series for K-4 students that speaks to 'the average' student from working and middle-class backgrounds. The spin evolves around real characters with idiosyncrasies and humor that embark on adventures. |
| Maggie Fern | Her spin and niche market is professional books for teachers that are hands-on and practical with a text design that can be used during classroom instruction. |

medium is the message" (McLuhan 1964). And since mobility, design, networked capacity, and volume of content are modern criteria for products, what defines spin continually changes over time.

## Case studies: the communicator, the novice, and the visionary

There is no *one* way to spin a product; every product has a multitude of possible spins. Nonetheless, there are patterns across interviews wherein some producers have more control or creative license over spin than other producers. Generally speaking, producers who work in corporations and corporate structures typically need to abide by company mandates, discourses, and agendas when designing products. What this means in practice is that texts produced in corporate environments have a company/corporation spin *and* the spin of the particular product. Moreover, such producers tend to work in collaboration with other, related departments. Marketing, sales, design, formatting, and distribution regularly meet about products and lines to collectively spin a story. Making it a group, collaborative endeavor has the twin effect of building on the expertise of others and having a collective investment in the product. The mobility of such a process, as in movement across departments, encourages creativity, teamwork, and innovation. Hence, an attendant disposition to spin is working collaboratively so that everyone has a say on what gets spun.

On the other side of the continuum are solo producers, who might consult with other professionals but who ultimately control the spin. Such individuals often build on the kudos of their successes and stake their reputation on a given aesthetic or imprint. Robin Benger, Twila Liggett, and Sarah Robinson are solo producers who carry with them a vision about film-making, children's television, and immersive environments (respectively). Their production vision guides the process, and they are frequently hired for a particular kind of spin that they give a product. Viewers recognize rhetorical, aesthetic, and substantive producer spins when they view texts. With film in mind, a viewer can easily differentiate a Woody Allen film from a Hitchcock or Tarantino film. The same is true for digital media; there is a look, sound, movement to digital media that signals certain designers.

There are three case studies featured in this section, where we illustrate the art of spin by looking at the idea the producer aims to bring to life; flagging the spin itself; and, examining the produced text (i.e. what it is, what it does, how it works). The first producer is Cassandra Mathers (pseudonym), Corporate Communications Manager for *Club Penguin*, where she handles public and media relations. A true advocate of the company, Cassandra showed her commitment to *Club Penguin* throughout the interview. From her perspective, *Club Penguin* gives children a truly safe, immersive environment, and her own experience as a mother is instantiated into her role as a communications manager for the company. This case study documents how digital media move from a grassroots company to a global phenomenon through spin.

The second producer is Kate Malone (pseudonym), a graduate student at Temple University who works on a design team to produce a website for adolescents called MyPopStudio.com as part of a research project on media literacy. As a member of a design team, Kate recounts 'aha' moments that she had during production that solidified MyPopStudio's spin. Kate also talks through ways of mediating teenage interests with the interests and needs of educators. This case study examines how a design team spins a research project into a virtual space.

The third producer is Twila Liggett (actual name), who produced the popular children's television show *Reading Rainbow* for 20 years with a team of experts. Driven by a passion and interest in education broadly and literacy education specifically, Twila typifies a maverick producer who has a different vision of children's educational programming. The story of *Reading Rainbow* illustrates how an innovative idea for television is spun into a national success story. This case study looks at a producer with a vision who works with a team to produce a television show.

### The communicator: Cassandra Mathers of Club Penguin

In autumn of 2007, we conducted a phone interview with Cassandra Mathers, who lives in British Columbia and works for a company called *Club Penguin*. Much of our interview revolves around the rise of the *Club Penguin* world from its beginnings in 2000 as a smaller, start-up company to its purchase by Disney in 2007 for $350 million. The story of *Club Penguin* is particularly appealing for us because of the product's popularity with children ages five to fourteen, an age-group that strongly appeals to producers of digital and new media because of the sheer number of users it implies.

The controlling idea for *Club Penguin* was to create an online playground, or sandbox, where children can play games, interact, and "hang out" as much as they do in real life. According to Cassandra, "the main motivator was to create a fun, safe place online for kids between the ages of six and fourteen to hang out and play games and interact with each other." In 2000, Lance Priebe launched *Club Penguin* as a virtual space with a design that used bright, primary colors and amorphous, friendly, cuddly penguin avatars. Yet, as Cassandra emphasizes, because of strict security measures and password protection, *Club Penguin* is less a website than a virtual space wherein children can safely interact with other penguin friends. *Club Penguin*'s spin is that children and even adolescents (because adolescents do use the site) are safer nowadays in the comfort and security of home playing in a virtual sandbox space rather than playing in a real sandbox or in community hubs where young people hang out. In 2007, there were 700,000 paid subscribers and 12 million activated users hanging out in *Club Penguin*'s virtual environment. Given the number of users documented using the site, it is clear that the idea and spun story had taken off.

Once users register as members, on the homepage, they create their own penguin personality however they see fit. Members create an identity for their penguin avatar by choosing a name, color, shape, accoutrements, and clothes, and even decorate their igloo to match their identities. After registering and establishing an identity for their penguin, members have access to many features in the "expansive *Club Penguin* world" (e.g. *Club Penguin* blog, interactive games, social networking on the main street, etc.). Also, there are products and "fun stuff" wherein members can submit artwork, comics, and cartoons to share with the *Club Penguin* community, as well as a quasi-Flickr space to share photos of penguins. There are game applications such as catching coffee bean bags or a music jam. A short film on the homepage tells members about the media ecology (Nardi and O'Day 2000) of *Club Penguin*, while a weekly newspaper entitled *The Club Penguin Times*, which "is key to the literacy aspect of *Club Penguin*," keeps users up-to-date on penguin events and newsworthy items. There is also an annual story-writing contest and a typing tutor game called "Paint by Letters," which is the first "intentionally educational type game" on the website. And to increase membership, members can participate in *Club Penguin* in multiple languages, including English, French, Spanish and, Portuguese.

The heart and soul of the *Club Penguin* world is the main street with a disco, coffee shop, and a store, where members can engage with one another through various activities and communities of practice (Lave and Wenger 1991).

Within a short walk of the main street, members of the site find a snow-capped outdoor play area where their penguin avatar meets up with other penguins to chat over a bonfire or throw a Frisbee or surf (see Figure 4.1).

As with any expansive world, *Club Penguin* offers so many features—from the blog, to picture sharing, to the newspaper—that the spun story of *Club Penguin* is more complex and hybrid than a simple virtual sandbox. Thus while the presiding spin remains a sandbox trope for social interaction, there are related spins within the ecology (Nardi and O'Day 2000) of the virtual world. Global awareness and citizenship, for instance, overlay the sandbox trope of *Club Penguin*; membership proceeds go to a program called "Coins for Change," which supports families in such countries as China, Ecuador, Kenya, and Ethiopia. Cassandra claims that "our Coins for Change program within the virtual world itself allows kids to donate virtual coins to help direct a real cash donation," reinforcing the sense of a community (at local and global levels) that takes care of each other. Although these aspects of the site appeal to children in reaching out to other children around the world, the philanthropic arm of the virtual world also appeals to parents because Coins for Change imbues a sense of citizenship, global awareness, and charitable practices in their children.

Club Penguin's spin underscores communication. For example, the newspaper, *The Club Penguin Times*, gives a sense that users can gravitate to different social networking features based on what they are looking for to construct a community and connect with others. It is this networked capacity that Cassandra stresses in our interview; to illustrate, she offers a story about a boy with Aspergers Syndrome as an example of how the *Club Penguin* world allows members, even those who may have difficulty interacting in-person, to communicate in a virtual forum:

*Figure 4.1* Snow-capped fun area in *Club Penguin*

> We spoke to a number of parents about the benefits for their children
> in specific situations in terms of social interaction . . . We have a little
> boy who is a member who has Aspergers, and his mom said what a
> great venue Club Penguin is for him to practice social interaction that
> may have negative repercussions in the real world, but he gets to try
> these things out in a place where people can't see him, or laugh at him,
> or make fun of him and it's a safe way to practice things that he can
> then practice in the real world . . . and that's what I think it offers kids,
> it's just another venue to do a lot of the things they are already doing,
> but it's just a safe, nurturing kind of venue . . .
>
> (2007)

By fostering social participation and social interaction for children who may feel
marginalized in real-life contexts, *Club Penguin* allows its users to blur their own
identities and create alternate identities with distinct characters, therein reinforcing the story of safety, comfort, acceptance, and even confidence.

Another layer of the participatory and social nature of *Club Penguin*—and a
strong appeal for parents—is the protection it offers children from both the
more benign hazards of internet use, such as spending too much time online,
and more sinister threats, like cyber-bullying and stalking. To ensure safety and

control over screen time, the *Club Penguin* team devised an egg-timer feature as part of the *Club Penguin* Parent Tools that "allows parents to monitor and limit when and how long his or her child can spend on *Club Penguin*, giving parents control over screen time." The egg-timer feature is up and running now (it was not at the time of the interview), thereby "allowing parents to have more control of and involvement in their child's online activities." Meanwhile, security filters are present through such features as live moderators and behind-the-scenes surveillance by the *Club Penguin* security team. All of these elements work together to create a spin for *Club Penguin* that keeps children coming back for more.

While *Club Penguin*'s spin rests on a belief that children today need safe hubs to meet up with friends and potential friends, the next producer talks about creating a safe space for teenagers.

### *The novice: Kate Malone of MyPopStudio.com*

Kate Malone (pseudonym), in her late twenties, is a mass media and communications doctoral student at Temple University. In addition to her own studies, Kate is involved with a larger research study at Temple University, working with a design team to produce a website called MyPopStudio.com, for adolescents and teenagers.

The website claims that: "The goal of the program is to transform girls' experiences with the media messages they see on TV and in magazines, on the radio, and on the web, moving away from simple and passive scanning towards a more active, cognitive, reflective and critical response. My Pop Studio 1) strengthens media literacy skills, 2) promotes positive youth development, and 3) increases knowledge about health issues." Yet, because the research study is funded by the Office of Women's Health (OWH), part of the US Department of Health and Human Services, a subtext of the website is developing young women's awareness of issues concerning women's health. The spin of the study is to teach based on media genres and through common digital practices. Coupled with an adolescent/younger generational spin, there is a spin for educators using the site as a support for their teaching. The site's spin is to create a digital environment where users not only strengthen media literacy skills and acquire information about health issues, but also develop some meta-awareness about how media works, practically and epistemologically.

To encourage users to develop critical awareness of media, the design team divided MyPopStudio into student domains with four areas of concentration: the music studio, the television studio, the magazine studio, and the digital studio, as well as a teacher and parent domain that offers lesson plans, activities, and curricular links. Within each domain, the site offers activities for users to play/complete. To spin the concept of media awareness, each media genre breaks apart what they do, say, and how they make users think.

Based on feedback that the design team received at the time of development, young women (the target audience) enjoy interactive games as a platform for

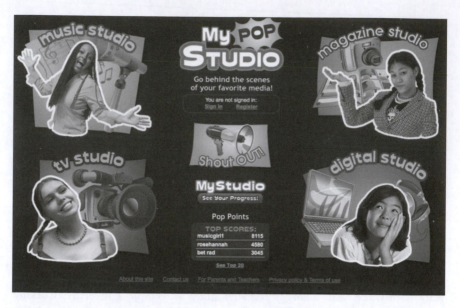

*Figure 4.2* MyPopStudio website

learning and understanding content and information. In response, the design team added paper-doll games, quizzes, and role-play games. As Kate explains, "one of the big things that we did was we added the ability to choose body sizing, so if you wanted the thin star, the average or larger one, and we had different skin tones, different hair styles and stuff and we tried to reflect a variety." By making the site game-based, producers achieved their goal of making the interface fun and interactive. The design blends visuals with photographs to give the design an accessible and, at the same time, sci-fi feel. Kate observes, "we wanted to be sci-fi and we wanted it to be sort of a genre that could appeal . . . what am I trying to say here . . . just didn't have a lot of gender and race implications, so our characters were like blue and orange." By making the interface sci-fi, the site obfuscates race, culture, and social class. The designers strategically represent different cultures and races through photos, as evident in an African-American woman in the music studio; a White-American or European woman in the television studio; an Asian woman in the digital studio; and a Hispanic woman in the magazine studio. Kate typifies a design-based approach to production in her recall of the design and redesign process.

To spin critical media awareness, the producers looked across media genres, foregrounding problem-solving and hidden skills and practices embedded in the enjoyment of digital texts and popular culture. In the music studio, for instance, users can create a pop star, reflect on and deconstruct song lyrics, and analyze how songs sell products. The website helps users deconstruct the rhetorical devices media producers use to sell products (i.e. the website analyzes spin). MyPopStudio encourages users to examine what each medium does and the skills

80

and practices used to understand them. In so doing, users interpret discursive and rhetorical devices and they experiment and improvise with skills used to understand television, magazines, and digital production. In each of the four studios MyPopStudio users interpret what each medium does and the knowledge systems instantiated in them. In the digital studio, users complete such activities as charting out a day in their life with comic-maker, therein operationalizing multi-tasking by playing a multi-tasking video game, and rewriting parts of their diary to encourage users to reflect on life events. In the television studio, users interpret televisual texts by engaging with characters and plot and finally, in the magazine studio, users deconstruct print media. By using comic-maker and fill-in-the-blank texts to simulate the kinds of practices readers engage in online, MyPopStudio raises awareness about what readers/users do when they engage with texts.

In spinning a story of critical media awareness, the website, according to Kate, "strengthens critical thinking skills," and the gaming motif complements those thinking activities through pedagogical support for teachers. In this way, the spun story rests as much on young people's contemporary literacy skills as it does on critically framing media and its virtues for teachers. Since interviewing Kate, the producers have added a "Shout Out" component, which is a blog where users can talk about movies, books, and games to expand the MyPopStudio world. There is a mixed message here. For example, while the studios cater to teenage females, offering applications that they know and like, the teacher pages cater to policy and curricular standards. The next producer we interviewed had a different philosophy for spinning literacy education, particularly reading, into something cool and edgy.

### The visionary: Twila Liggett of Reading Rainbow

Twila Liggett had several roles before producing *Reading Rainbow*. Having been a teacher, grant writer, and consultant, she gradually came to appreciate that "media is an enabler of literacy" and as such, needs to be harnessed to inspire interest in books and reading at a young age. With the credo of "media as an enabler," Twila designed and produced the Emmy award-winning, 23-years-in-the-running show, *Reading Rainbow*.

In July 1983, *Reading Rainbow* was aired, running five days a week throughout the year as a way of "subverting reading loss." In devising the show, Twila had two main motives: first, to make a difference in education by using television as an enabler of learning; and, second, to use her grant-writing skills to get funding for dynamic, high-budget episodes that went beyond an existing model of educational children's programming that, in Twila's words, was so boring, "you had to nail kids' feet to the ground" to watch it. She also had two convictions about the spin of the show. The first was that she "didn't want it to be didactic," vowing that she would not reproduce the same staid format that existed at the time and that she would make the show innovative and edgy. Her second conviction was that she "would surround [her]self with the brightest and the best in the business." Her hand-picked production team, which includes an academic, professional producers who had been involved in popular children's television such as *Sesame Street*, and LeVar Burton as the host, completed her picture of the brightest and the best.

Born out of these two convictions, the controlling idea of *Reading Rainbow* was always to make reading look as interesting and enticing as possible and, as Twila expressed it, "to celebrate bookness." To transform the idea into a spin, Twila shaped the spin in collaboration with the *Reading Rainbow* team. By producing a series that offered a male, African-American host, books as the centerpiece, and ways of extending stories into real-life situations, Twila produced a show so different that it revolutionized children's television.

Before *Reading Rainbow*, shows were primarily based on a read-aloud model wherein a host, usually female, would read a picture book to children. *Reading Rainbow* strove to go into the world of a book's story to bring its story into the real world by applying it to actual contexts and actual people; the fantasy-reality trope of going around the New York area or including popular cultural icons such as Kermit the Frog and Run DMC made the show look quite different from its contemporaries. In an executive summary, which Twila wrote years after *Reading Rainbow* was in production, she described the innovative approach the show took:

> The *Reading Rainbow* approach is based in its essence on the sound and widely proven precept that reading aloud to children is the single most important factor in aiding their literacy development and predicting future school achievement (Snow, Burns, and Griffin, 1998). Of equal importance, by making reading and literature fun and engaging, and existing in the real world, *Reading Rainbow* also provides young children with motivation for an interest in books, reading, and learning. This factor has been seen (Csikszentmihalya, 1990) as a powerful influence on the development of an appreciation of the rewards of literacy.
>
> (Executive summary by Twila Liggett, December 2000)

Admittedly, Twila wrote the executive summary in hindsight of the show's development, but there was a definite melding of traditional literacy research with an innovative, multimodal approach when the idea was spun into a television show. Reading as multimodal—as a practice that demands an understanding of the written word as much as it demands an understanding of oral language and visuals—was ahead of its time when *Reading Rainbow* came on the scene. Yet the effect was a hit. Much like the safety of social networking on *Club Penguin*, *Reading Rainbow* affected the way in which children felt about books and worlds within books, and modes were primarily responsible, as evident in the consistent connection made between the printed word and sounds through music. In one particular episode, LeVar Burton read *Zin! Zin! Zin! A Violin* and then featured on-location footage with the Juillard School of Music's Chamber Orchestra at the Lincoln Centre. In another episode, there was a different mode used wherein LeVar and Kermit the Frog danced to music to illustrate parts of a book, demonstrating content through the mode of movement. By relying on the book and its story world, read-alouds, and content coming to life in familiar places, Twila's vision of *Reading Rainbow* placed "high-quality books centre stage." In the wake of the show, creating related story extensions, for both fiction and non-fiction, became an accepted approach on television to literacy teaching and learning.

LeVar Burton completed the innovative tapestry of *Reading Rainbow* in that he defied what hosts of children's television shows looked and sounded like at the time of its launch. Although LeVar was not a cast member of Star Trek when he began as host of *Reading Rainbow*, he became a cast member during its production, and his role enhanced his stature as different and cutting-edge. Twila talked about the pivotal moment when LeVar joined the *Reading Rainbow* team: "I wanted a male host from the beginning. I had said I'm only going to look at males, that's the plan here . . . and then someone saw LeVar and I thought, what a good message that is, a verbal, well-spoken African-American host." LeVar materializes an innovative, outside-of-the-box spin to *Reading Rainbow*, and his much-quoted, iconic phrase, "But you don't have to take my word for it; read for yourself," became a catch-line for children who watched *Reading Rainbow* every day.

As *Reading Rainbow* illustrates, television spin is different from digital spin, primarily because television is more static; that is, viewers had limited access

*Figure 4.3* LeVar Burton on *Reading Rainbow*. *Reading Rainbow* is available on DVD at http://shopdei.com.

to texts. Moreover, televisual texts demand nuanced characterization, such as LeVar in *Reading Rainbow*.

## Conclusion: pulling back the curtain on spin

Finding a voice in writing is much like finding the right spin for a product. Matching structure, discourse and register to the genre, a potential reader requires a similar thoughtful regard for choices to materialize ideas and thoughts. Spin is our contemporary writer's voice and it needs to be more transparent for students to understand the difference between an okay spin and the right spin. Given that multimodal composition demands an understanding of design and graphic principles, there needs to be an expansion of concepts used when teaching "writing" in school. Case studies in the chapter illustrate how producers forge dispositions focused on hitting the audience with the right message through the right text.

Though multimodal compositions such as virtual environments, movies, and television shows have become our prime vehicle for the dissemination of information and means of connecting with others, school literacy still rests on mastering the written word through argument or tone and other print-ruled dispositions. Though there have been strides in literacy education by examining other genres of texts and using technology as a teaching support, there are obvious gaps in the way that producers of communication think and the way that communication is taught in-school. Shifting mindsets, or even simply taking up some different ones that are more in line with design literacies and digital environments, is a way forward for literacy pedagogy and curriculum. Perhaps even incorporating such concepts as color, perspective, shapes, angles, patterns, and motifs in texts are ways of opening up writing pedagogy. Foregrounding the affordances of modes and ways of spinning them represents a way of making literacy more ideological, more fluid, and more based on social interaction.

As human creations, television shows, websites, and video games are never objective or anonymous. The silent voices and practices evident in the three case studies are etched in texts that they design. During a production process, workplace contexts enculturate ways of being and rules that are naturalized into texts, affecting not only what gets produced, but also how audiences take up these rules and generate their own thinking through them. To truly understand a website, a children's book, a television show and so on, users and viewers need to understand not just its linguistic, cultural, social, and economic embeddedness, but also how all of these forces are brought together in a text and what set of hands is involved in their making. When we think about the producers in these and subsequent cases, a language and epistemology emerge that tell a story about how we communicate. An understanding both of what that language looks like and the frameworks for thinking in terms of design literacies can help students, teachers, and even policy-makers create participatory structures to think in multimodal ways.

# 5

# MODES SPINNING STORIES

They actually put a girl animator on Olivia, she's twenty-four her
name is _____, they um put Aretha Franklin's "Respect," and
you know literally they just did one test of Olivia in her little red
pajamas walking, and it was just a movement and it was a movement just like with anybody else when you just go, wow like that
spunk, that spontaneous, and it's just like you know wow, bam . . .
and so it's just like a dance choreography or when an actor comes
in for a scene and they have that presence, and they nail the character, they nail the character through the walk cycle. She didn't
say anything, she just walked and she had a little smile on her
face and she had her little walk and we were in love.
                    (Megan Laughton, Chorion Creative Director, 2008)

In describing her first reaction to Nickelodeon's animated character Olivia,
Megan identifies the effect that an artful manipulation of modes can have on
an audience. Where the previous chapter looked at spin as an action or practice producers engage in, this chapter looks at the elements producers use to
create spin. Recognizing that there are multiple ways to spin a story, this chapter examines choices in modes of representation that shape what gets told. This
is a book about a new, fresh way of viewing meaning making from the perspectives of insiders in the production industry. As such, the book takes for granted
that modes other than language are prominent. By examining modes in detail
and by analyzing three producer texts and their descriptions of text production,
we offer ways that teachers can think about how modes tell stories.

  With inexpensive digital cameras flooding the market, and a proliferation of
websites like YouTube hosting unlimited numbers of clips, it has never been
easier to be a producer of digital media. Yet, while technologies make it possible for anyone to be a producer, the choices a person makes and the modes
a person selects to bring an idea to life separate one producer from another.
What choices and resources do professional producers have at their disposal?
What decisions do producers face when determining the best way to represent
an idea? How do their choices affect the text that they create, and by extension,

the story audiences experience? In this chapter, we aim to answer these questions by looking at modes available to—and privileged by—producers, and the ways a producer's choices for getting at "the core essence" spin stories in multimodal texts.

## Modes

Modes have been described in a variety of ways: "stuff" (Kress 1997); "a heuristic unit" (Norris 2004); "a regularized organized set of resources for meaning-making" (Jewitt and Kress 2003: 1). The essence of what modes do is the substantive *and* aesthetic work for texts. Modes physically realize what producers want/need to transmit. In general, these channels of representation might include writing, speech, gestures, and practices used to convey and understand texts. It is a picture that says what words cannot say; it is a sound that resurrects thoughts, emotions, or sentiments in the listener; it is the manner in which an English teacher moves around a classroom when teaching Shakespeare (Kress et al. 2005); and it is an animated sequence at the beginning of a website. Through these and other elements, modes both show and tell the story. While traditional, linear, one-dimensional texts may rely on conventional modes such as words and visuals, multimodal texts draw on multiple modes to convey their message/s. Certainly multimodal texts such as web pages or video games may include conventional text modes, say writing or pictures, but they might also include color schemes, layout, characterization, interactivity, or hyperlinks, as well as less tangible elements such as structuring conditions and contexts. By understanding the modes a producer can select—and those a producer ultimately selects to represent ideas—we can better understand the knowledge and practices needed to compose and communicate multimodally.

## Modal choice

The earliest known attempts at making meaning with modes date back to 30,000 AD with wall drawings or pictographs followed by more intricate and complex drawings called ideographs. These drawings capture a sense of the time and entrenched practices, such as hunting for animals. Fast forward to thousands of years later in 1440, when Gutenberg introduced printing with ink on paper and books were handwritten by scribes. Designed to imitate the kinds of letters religious scribes wrote at the time, the printed word, our primary means of communication, took hold for centuries. Fast forward again to 2009, when production happens in digital media and printing operates from computers and the use of UV inks. In other words, our history reminds us that modes of representation have consistently depicted stories, and it is only the types of modes and our access to them that have become more sophisticated and varied. Even typing a Word document demands modal choice and materiality to spin a message: choosing a font, putting in headers or footers, situating page numbers, bolding heads and subheads and so on. There are choices to be made and these choices express intended meanings. There is nothing new or revelatory in noting this, yet, continual, habitual choosing of modes and the enactment of designs does not guide literacy pedagogy. Professional producers, however, treat modal decisions as pivotal to the success or failure of a product.

Aesthetics, structure, visuals, and movement express the interest and motivation of the producer (Kress 1997). As noted earlier, questions arise in the midst of modal choice: Will a sound transmit a message or should it be coupled with a photograph? Will a word scrolled across a computer screen entice a viewer? What kind of font suits a publication? Will it be serif or sans serif? It is so commonplace for producers to contemplate the minutiae of modal choice, that it is second-nature.

Modal choice can therefore be regarded as a way of thinking through how a story needs to be told. Our producers taught us this lesson about production, and they serve, ultimately, as the best example to illustrate the point. For instance, Rachel Hurdley (actual name), one of our producers, helped to produce a 15-minute film for an Economic and Social Research Council Grant (ESRC) with Bella Dicks entitled, *Watching, Listening, Reading, Clicking: Representing Qualitative Research in Different Media*, wherein she learned, the hard way, to think multimodally. Her journey conducting the research and making a short film illustrates a movement from print logic to multimodal logic, and epiphanies that happen along the way.

Coming from a background in material culture and cultural studies, Rachel became a part of the research in-process when she was given the task of editing down hours of footage into a 15-minute film about an interactive discovery centre in Wales, UK called Technaquest. Committed to imbuing an ethnographic perspective into the 15-minute film, Rachel strove to embed an ethnographic eye into the editing process by focusing on "allowing participants to speak" and to share "an all-round view of any social event or situation." Rachel came into the film's production after all of the footage had been filmed, and she had 35 hours of footage that she had to whittle down to 15 minutes. Having little experience with producing films, Hurdley forged a partnership with a BBC film editor who has worked on such shows as *Doctor Who*, a popular television show in the UK.

The process comprised a series of epiphanies for Rachel in that it made her realize that she thinks in terms of writing, which is not the same as thinking filmicly; in our interview she claimed: "you can't think about this as writing, what we have to do is view all the original footage and the communication of the argument will come from that." To retain original voices and to obfuscate a narratorial presence, Rachel had to find moments when visuals *and* audio were strong. According to Nick (BBC Editor), it is possible to rescue bad pictures, but you cannot rescue bad sound. As a result, Rachel and Nick watched endless footage with the criteria that "to make good film, you need good sound [Rachel quoting Nick]." If the film was to remain truly ethnographic, with no narratorial voice-over, then they had to cut all clips with bad sound (most of the footage had poor sound due to the nature of recording). Given Rachel's journey into production, thinking filmicly was tantamount to thinking about affordances and constraints of modes and the most innovative and technically astute way of communicating ideas. Working with multimedia requires operating in terms of multiple modes.

In Table 5.1, we list dominant modes producers in our study use, ordered from concrete, accepted modes, such as written words and visuals, to more abstract, invisible modes, such as hypertext and spatial dimensions and proximity.

Building on Table 5.1, modes can add light, texture, mood, majesty and other atmospheric effects, depending on what a producer wants to achieve; a mode's impact in one medium may be completely different in another. While a mode's intention derives from what a producer wishes to represent, its effect emerges from the social situation the text is intended for, meaning what and how the producer's representation can best speak to that situation. Going back to Rachel's story, to blur the narratorial voice, the producers focused on strong visual and audio moments of participants at Technaquest, so that the listener focused on the participants in the film and not on the narrator. Considering forms of representation and reception of text points to two fundamental aspects of mode: choice and materiality. For the former, choice, producers featured in this and other chapters have to think about the best mode or combination of modes to express their meaning/spun story. For the latter, materiality, producers need to think about how those choices will be received by the viewer depending on the medium in which viewers receive a message (McLuhan 1964). In the research, we focus on how producers use modes to emphasize that physical features in texts such as color choice are content, and they are read as content, as opposed to being thought of as dressing up content or as being a design feature. This is why students as multimodal producers need a language and literacy framework that uses *multi*modal logic.

As a final note about modal choice, synaesthesia plays a role in what modes producers choose. In *Before Writing* (1997), Gunther Kress unravels the concept that modes need to "feel right" (39) for a text. In his account of two drawings by a six-year-old girl and eight-year old boy, Kress talks about how both meaning-makers produced drawings that depict "the iconography of Halloween" (39) by privileging the same mode, color, but in quite different ways. The girl's text presents light, happy figures, and she employs bright orange, blue, red, and green to exude lightness and levity, but in the boy's text, he presents a darker mood with heavy, black lines and small splashes of color. Kress's analysis of the drawings throws into relief how modal choice draws on a producer's translation of mood in modes chosen to depict a message. He describes what an "entirely common human characteristic" (39) it is to present moods and feelings through modes that feel right to the meaning-maker in the moment of production. To extend his message, Kress talks about how suppressed this synaesthetic quality is in school, where there is a "preference for writing-centred work." Producers in

*Table 5.1* Modes and their effects

| Mode | Effect |
| --- | --- |
| Written words | Say what other modes cannot say through words read by readers/viewers. Words can be direct or indirect and can be shaped around the register of a given genre, allowing users to understand, claim, speculate, and assert linguistically and literally. |
| Visuals | Realize materially what words, sounds, and gestures cannot express. Visuals speak to synaesthetic, somatic feelings that cast an impression of the story behind the text effect. |
| Sound | Conjures up thoughts, ideas, values, and memories in the listener's mind, adding an emotional subtext. |
| Color | Sets the mood and tone of a story; for example, bold, primary colors emit a lively, perhaps more child-like ethos, whereas muted or monochromatic colors imbue a sedate, serious tone. Although some people may see color as a visual, it is in fact a separate mode. |
| Photography | Captures moments and freezes them as visible cultural forms, bringing together several modes—color, movement, visuals, angles—in a single text. Like color, photographs can be mistaken for visual modes, but they are a separate mode that carries particular effects. Photographs can be aerial giving an effect of a panorama, or they can close-in on a person capturing a mood or personal trait. Photographers offer an interpretation of someone or something by framing pictures through angles and vectors. |
| Interactivity | Allows users to interact or transact (Rosenblatt 1995) with texts. For example, users can write back and forth as producers on blogs, wikis, chatrooms, social networking spaces, and interactivity "permits the user to enter into an entirely new relation with all other texts—the notion of hypertextuality" (Kress 2003: 5). |
| Hypertextuality | Connects ideologically and substantively to other related texts, implying sponsorships (Brandt 2001). Multisemiotic mediation in hypertext uses different semiotic resources to engage viewers. Often involving two modes dominating the story of a text simultaneously. |

our study pull on synaesthesia to produce multimodal compositions. Feeling right about modal choice and experimenting with design until a design materializes an idea is a disposition that many of our interviewees talked about when they reflected on producing a text. In order to illustrate modal choice, materiality and synaesthesia, we present three case studies of producers and their modal choices.

## Case studies: the storyteller, the editor, and the historian

Because modes tell stories, looking closely at modes directs us to a central point about literacy: identifying the right mode to tell the story. This chapter takes this concept to heart by documenting producers' stories of modal representation. The first case study features Robin Benger (actual name), an award-winning documentary film-maker, who was possibly the most eloquent of our producers on the issue of choosing modes to express meanings. The second case study is Jonathon Gravings (pseudonym), a news editor at CNN, who provided a technical view of what happens in corporate contexts when choosing the right mode. Finally, Patricia Mavo (actual name), a historian, particularly interested in oral history, who seeks to imbue her philosophy of oral history into digital media, provides a telling case of someone who embeds a particular perspective into digital media. The fact is that every one of our producers selects modes that affect and effect messages that they want or need to convey. An analysis of modes highlights how modal choice is shaped by genre and text medium and how choices differ across mediums which can help educators identify a language for experimenting with modes to complete assignments.

### *The storyteller: Robin Benger of Cogent/Benger Productions*

Robin Benger has been making documentaries for over 30 years and is committed to documentary film-making as "a medium of mass story telling." We interviewed Robin in his studio in Toronto. Over the course of the interview, Robin describes the origins of his production philosophy, growing up in South Africa and then England. Given his ties to South Africa and living through Apartheid, Robin's documentaries transmit his passion for activism with an earnest desire for tolerance of cultures and overall "peace and good order." In addition to the documentaries detailed in this case study, Robin has produced documentaries on such wide-ranging topics as cricket, Paul Anka, wolverines, and illegal immigrants. Robin shared production stories of two of his documentaries with us, *Madiba: The Life and Times of Nelson Mandela* and *First Person Shooter*.

Born in South Africa, Robin moved to the UK and lived there for some time before moving and settling in Canada. Robin views production as a way of casting an impression on a viewer. To be specific, modes enable him to take a stance. Choices in mode shift, based on his perspective on the topic. When discussing cricket and its evolution over time, Robin talks about choosing a mode that might express this perspective. When producing a radio program broadcast across Canada, Robin accounts for how it will be heard in a variety of places, such as on a boat in Newfoundland, or in the far reaches of a prairie province. Such intricate accounts of text reception and design are a part of Robin's philosophy of film-editing.

When Robin chooses a dominant mode for his productions, he seeks out ways of achieving an effect. Robin has a phrase that he used in our interview that encapsulates using a mode to materialize an effect, and he called the effect an "evocative detail": "So what is really going on behind the mass image? I was really encouraged to dig, but in terms of structuring the evocative detail, something that would take the ordinary story way beyond the everyday." Robin's choice of mode relies on the nature of the content, but what modes do in Robin's productions is exude an evocative detail that he wants to get across. In other words, evocative details materialize the message of a text. An effect relies on the notion of synaesthesia, because it rests on how viewers respond to the text (on a felt, emotional level). Robin wields modes as a stimulus for senses. For instance, a sound hints of a memory, or a camera angle implies a mood. For Robin, modes afford certain kinds of meanings and he uses modes for atmospheric effects in his work.

During our interview, Robin dwelled on the topic of how to structure multimodal production. On the topic of structure, Robin talks about modal choice and materialization and also modal constraints. That is, Robin has produced a variety of multimodal texts from radio shows to films to, more recently, digital texts. With each one, Robin uses a presiding mode often coupled with other modes to get across his message. Yet, with each medium in which he works, he acknowledges that he takes account of how the text will be received. To account for constraints and variable conditions by which a text is heard or viewed, Robin describes a production practice that he employs to test out different listening contexts and modal constraints:

> We would play back the documentary on this little box, this old-fashioned tape recorder with a terrible speaker because the theory was that a farmer's wife in rural Saskatchewan or a fisherman on his boat off Nova Scotia would have a little radio and would need to hear clearly the story.
>
> (2007)

Taking account of modal constraints became a part of his reasoning and disposition as a producer. Also, in the early days of his career, Robin recalls structuring his content "in a linear fashion," which remained an abiding philosophy, because of his training at the CBC where he got a story on Monday, traveled to far reaches and enemy lines until Friday, and assembled and edited footage for a Sunday morning broadcast. Time, length, audience, and discourses shape Robin's modal choices and the semiotic resources that he chooses to produce the footage.

The first documentary that illustrates Robin's use of modes is a documentary that he produced on the life and times of Nelson Mandela. From the beginning of the interview, it is clear that Robin's South African roots anchored the production of this award-winning film, *Madiba: The Life and Times of Nelson Mandela*. The film moves from Mandela's life leading up to his imprisonment and ends with his freedom. In a website describing the making of *Madiba*, Robin talks about a motivating factor behind his film work, and that is an image of a child that depicts the simultaneous loneliness and marginalization coupled with freedom, justice, and liberation that he experienced in South Africa:

> When I make my films I think of a ten-year-old child somewhere in the far reaches of this country and beyond, watching, learning, looking for guidance. This story about Nelson Mandela is accessible to all but directed to that ten year old. That there is a way to overcome great loneliness and marginalisation; to bring freedom and justice and liberation to millions of people who don't have it. That's what Nelson Mandela did. This documentary is an attempt to show what happened.
>
> (Benger n.d.)

In many of his films, especially in *Madiba*, Robin wants to depict emotions that he felt as a child and that are still a reality in South Africa. Loneliness, imprisonment, marginalization and, at the same time, freedom, justice, and liberation are all present in the film through Robin's choices of images, camera angles, sound and movement. One mode Robin chose to convey loneliness and liberation is sound. The movie begins with the sound of a dripping faucet and the dripping faucet represents the desolate prison cell and fetid conditions of imprisonment. The idea of a dripping faucet derived from stories his friend Steve Bartlice shared about what prison life is like in Africa; Bartlice had memories of a dripping faucet in a Ugandan prison where he spent time as a youth, imprisoned for his activist work. Bartlice's descriptions stayed with Robin and became a way to materialize emotions that he wanted to run throughout the production and that he could not replicate with visuals or words. Robin describes how he identified the mode and used it to his advantage in the film:

> . . . he was taken into torture . . . sort of a basement in some big building I forget, but some big building where the people were taken and tortured and there was a dripping tap [faucet], and he would call this the dripping tap, and you know the sound of a dripping tap but he used it as a descriptive phrase but I forget what it was, but it just brought the whole audience into that scene of the horror.
>
> (2007)

Herein we see how a mode materializes an idea, becoming an audio metaphor for the message. In this way, the insidious nature of the dripping faucet heard for years on end reminds the viewer of a sacrifice that Mandela made in the name of peace and freedom in his country. The dripping faucet recollects Steve Bartlice's haunting description of Ugandan prison life, it is the sound that exudes a feeling in Benger's documentary. Benger transmits a feeling through audio that evokes isolation, pain, suffering, thereby sending out powerful messages about the conditions under which Mandela endured prison life.

Much of our interview with Robin evolved around the making and aftermath of *First Person Shooter*, a documentary that depicts Robin's realization that his 11-year-old son is addicted to video games and the implications of that addiction. Where *Madiba* uses sound with visuals and a voice-over to convey the message of the film, *First Person Shooter* uses visuals combined with camera angles to depict the film's message.

Robin devoted a year of his life to work solely on *First Person Shooter*, and, at the beginning of our interview, there is some detachment about the production as an exposé of the video game industry. As the interview progresses, however, it becomes clear that the documentary also recounts Robin's struggles with his son Griffin's addiction to the war game, *Counter-Strike*. The impact of Griffin's story visually threaded in the documentary and manifested in the image of Robin heading down the basement steps, taking footage along the way, captures how disturbed he felt by Griffin and his friends engrossed in battle in front of flashing screens. The room is dark and the camera moves from a cavernous basement to Griffin's face fixed on the screen as seen in Figure 5.1.

*Figure 5.1* Griffin engrossed in game battle

Just as the dripping faucet in *Madiba* evokes a response from a viewer, so too the darker footage, the bright, mesmerizing computer screens, the transfixed looks of teenagers as they stare at the screen help audiences understand the sense of horror that Robin felt every time he saw Griffin absorbed in game-play. He talks about this painful period during our interview:

> Well, *First Person Shooter* was unique because I never brought myself into my own documentaries, and I hadn't thought about doing a documentary about my family . . . but my son, my oldest son, I have three kids, I'm guessing he was around the age of 11. I'm going to say, he was the apple of our eye . . . he was a very good sportsman, very good at school, and very bright . . . and maybe this is more information than you need but it was sort of unconditional love . . . he became completely, I use the word addicted by this one video game called *Counter-Strike*, and I tried also some things at home, from the tough to the understanding to try to peel him away from this game, and his friends, all of them were coming over and that's all they wanted to do was play this game and, as you see in the documentary, it starts with literally one day I have this little hand held camera with me. I took it down into the basement to see the shot, and I decided to go into the world of video games . . . I stopped all my projects and I was doing things independent for twelve years you know I was doing a bunch of things, and I stopped everything and decided this was going to be my professional life for the next year . . .
>
> (2007)

For his part, Robin recounts the whole experience with a producer's detachment, but clearly our interview dialogue highlights how *First Person Shooter* is a personal account of Robin's struggles with his son. While much of the documentary involves discussions about the gaming industry, going to conventions and interviewing people involved with video game design and production, the scenes where Robin walks down the basement steps to find his son playing video games, make the documentary an intimate look at how a parent discovers and comes to terms with his son's addiction.

Others also noticed the biographical nature of the film. When Robert completed two-thirds of the footage for *First Person Shooter*, he said that the CTV producer that sponsored its production made an insightful observation about the central storyline of his documentary:

> the producer of the show said, this is about your son and you, this is a documentary about you and your son . . . and I was like oh my god because seeing myself on camera really distorts the whole directorial thing . . . but the actual fact, I created an actual character on film who was the father, and that's how I was able to do it . . . I was the father, I

was the director, and I was the father of the son . . . yet you mostly see my back.

(2007)

Robin was aware of his activist ways and his desire to spread a message of peace and tolerance. Yet, what he did not see in *First Person Shooter* is the biographical nature of the documentary juxtaposed with his other productions. That is, *First Person Shooter* depicts the vulnerability and isolation that Robin felt when he witnessed his son's obsession with a shooter game. And once a colleague pointed out this dimension of the film, Robin admits how blind-sided he felt by the experience:

> Well, it was very awkward and very unsettling doing *First Person Shooter* because it was just about me and my son and I wanted it to be a public issue, and it went against my nature but, then again, in retrospect, we all survived it all pretty well.

(2007)

Suddenly, it is obvious that our discussion moves from analyzing his documentary about the adverse effects of video games on young people to a story about his painful experience with his son. In some ways, *First Person Shooter* is a production about his own story, trying to remain objective and omniscient during the production only to realize that it is a subjective and deeply personal production about him and his son.

Through visuals of Griffin interwoven with sound bites of *Counter-Strike* battles, Robin's documentary is a motivated sign (Kress 1997) in that it pulls on our senses to express Robin's desire to portray his struggles with Griffin. *First Person Shooter* materializes innate dispositions, histories, and unravels a past further back even than Griffin's birth, back to when Robin was a young boy in South Africa during Apartheid. For the longest time Robin made documentaries to be subversive or send across a message, yet in this instance, his own story is the message.

As a producer, Robin is adept at identifying what mode dominates his text to transmit a value or idea, and evoking emotions is a producer practice particularly strong within his philosophy of production. The next case study stands in contrast with Robin in that he is ruled less by evoking emotions and more by drawing on technical acumen and an ability to "impact images" during production.

### The editor: Jonathon Gravings of CNN Broadcasting

Jonathon Gravings is a news editor at CNN who lives and works in New York City. Having completed a film and production degree at Rutgers University's Mason Gross School, Jonathon interned at MTV before landing a position at

CNN as a news editor. Jonathon has aspirations to be a film-maker and, in fact, is presently involved in producing some independent films. Jonathon offered us a picture of life in a large news broadcasting corporation.

Jonathon, a breed of media producer seen in media hubs like New York City, puts in long hours designing media texts that speak across audiences. Committed to the art of editing, he will work for hours to capture the right image for a story. In this way, Jonathon tells stories through visuals; in his words: "a big component to production is really trying to tell a story through pictures." Of the three producers showcased in the chapter, Jonathon is the most technical in the manner in which he talks about his vocation. As he describes it, "we just spend a lot of time in editing rooms just trying to figure out what's the best shot." Although Jonathon has formal training in film editing, he learned most of his trade working at MTV and CNN; he describes the immersion process as follows, "it's just really trying to get a grasp of it by immersing myself in the process in terms of doing the research to see how others have done it [i.e. exposing myself to people who have done it or are in the process of doing it]."

Adopting an apprenticeship model exposes him to different models of production such as those at MTV and those at CNN. Yet, like Robin, Jonathon believes that what production boils down to is story-telling:

> It's kind of an enhancement of the experience. As an editor here at CNN, I am putting together stories, I am pulling full shows together for broadcast . . . and you have to be able to see what is most effective in the stories that you are telling. I effect images . . .
>
> (2007)

"To effect images" entails garnering the most powerful impact. To create a given message, Jonathon works within the constraints of a CNN production, which can include shortened schedules, deadlines, and interruptions when juggling multiple projects. Given that CNN airs human interest and news stories, Jonathon's example offers insight into how producers work within news broadcasting corporation constraints and, at the same time, maintain an artistic and technical vision about multimodal composition.

Jonathon is attuned to subtle shifts in the effect of different modes in texts. As a genre, human-element stories tend to have more images with less voice-over and more sound, and news items tend to have images with sound bites about what the news item depicts. These hidden, on-the-ground producer concepts preside over Jonathon's philosophy of production.

In our conversation, we returned to visuals, "effecting images," "finding the right footage," and giving a spin to material through modal choice. Jonathon is more literal than Robin when he discusses how he chooses visuals and photography that work with sound rather than talking, like Robin, about visuals as metaphoric. CNN is news all of the time with a reputation of being the first broadcaster to cover a news item, and, during the interview, Jonathon kept coming back to the fact that being on a CNN team means tight timelines and making news items as dynamic as possible though, at times, limited in terms of modalities. That is, Jonathon's choices for materializing new footage are limited to resources he has at-hand (e.g., whether live footage is available or not). This kind of spontaneous improvising appeared to be what excited Jonathon most about the production process.

In addition to time and resource constraints, CNN producers have to be attentive to other, evolving media that attract their target audience such as weblogs and YouTube:

> It's no longer just traditionally whether it's just you're watching it on a TV screen as such, a lot of people are viewing their stuff on a computer now and so that is even affecting things on a larger broadcast level. We're starting to have to look at alternate ways of reaching our audience so we start to put more emphasis on things like podcasts and YouTube debates. It's about evolving with it otherwise you get left behind.
>
> (2007)

Moving with technologies means that Jonathon needs to broaden his editing practices to encompass other genres; in our discussion, this trend prompted Jonathon to elaborate on moments of multimodal compositions in detail. As an example of choosing the right mode to materialize an effect, Jonathon discussed footage he edited on a Minnesota bridge collapse. In 2007, there was a Minnesota bridge collapse, and the only resources that Jonathon had at the time of the production were still images of the collapse—no live footage, no on-the-scene account, just pictures, sound bites and a voice-over:

> I remember that we did something on the Minnesota bridge collapse where all I had was a bunch of still photos of the events and it's like, well, I have to put a two-minute piece together for air tonight, for the show that night and it's like, "well, I don't have any video. All you've given me were still pictures, and so how do you make that into an experience that you can bring to the audience member?"
>
> (2007)

The default, dominant mode in this production was still photographs, which Jonathon combined with sound to guide the viewer into an interpretation of horror and devastation. In our longest, sustained conversation, Jonathon talked about spinning a story around the bridge collapse. For the footage, photographs effected images by exploiting the emotive power of color in photos from the fire. That is, color helped express the horror, the "flash and boom" of the fire, the bold reds and golds of the flames made the strongest impact in the news feature. Jonathon's nuanced understanding of modes foregrounds the disposition of experimentation as a learned, important practice in production. By choosing color in photographs coupled with sound, Jonathon recreated the drama of the scene for the audience, just as the next research participant captures personal history through color and photographs.

### The historian: Patricia Mavo of American Life Publishers

Patricia lives and works in Florida, and we interviewed her through a series of email exchanges. A few years ago, Patricia shifted from graduate work in history to learning web design. Like Jonathon Gravings, Patricia Mavo opts for visuals and photographs over other modes in production work, but she uses these modes for different reasons and to achieve a very different effect. Claiming that she is a historian first and web designer second, Patricia came into digital media with a desire to embed her passion for history, more specifically, oral history into digital designs, as exemplified by her work on a website for Oral Heritage Productions.

Oral Heritage Productions's mission is to chronicle individuals' oral histories in the form of transcriptions or short films or photo-scanning restoration, or whatever medium in which an individual would like to capture their family's history. Oral Heritage Productions aims to create a website to help people capture their past. Patricia's expertise in oral history and her skill as a digital designer matched Oral Heritage Productions's mission perfectly. To promote oral history, Patricia sought ways "to educate and to promote the preservation of personal histories in order to ensure that families, businesses, and historians have a more comprehensive picture of history than what we have had in the past." Patricia materializes this preservation of personal histories through modal choice. Arguing that "history has to be tangible" for people to relate to it, Patricia designed the website with authentic photographs of children and families together in bygone and contemporary times. In Figures 5.2 and 5.3, there are real-life photographs from the website that give it a local feel inviting viewers to think about their own family history.

Photographs exude history either through objects as symbols such as a shadow of a tree or through authentic photographs of married couples as in Figure 5.2 or recent pictures of grandchildren as in Figure 5.3. Part of Patricia's design and aesthetic is a depiction of diversity within families, which is clear in Figure 5.3.

Patricia wanted photographs that were racially and culturally diverse. Patricia maintains that "all the photos on the website were chosen to represent our diversity as human beings, but they are also uniquely western-hemispheric and local because that is my audience and I want photos to appeal to them and be familiar." When asked about the relationship between photos and oral history Patricia observes as follows: "one stimulates our auditory senses and the other, our visual. I want you to imagine someone in the photo telling or finishing their story." To that end, she uses visuals to stimulate user imagination. In so doing, Patricia compels users of the site to think about how they might present their own family history.

*Figure 5.2*
Married couple
from the past

*Figure 5.3* Photo of culturally
diverse families

Like Jonathon's discussion about color in the fire footage, Patricia talks about how color in the Oral Heritage Productions website imbues an emotion and memories:

> I completely felt the browns and creams as history—as if the gentle aging of pictures or paper . . . I also had that feel with the images. In the same way that the trees felt like an old-fashioned notion of time—of a stroll, perhaps down memory lane. Half of the photos are from my own personal family history.
>
> (Email exchange, 2007)

Colors, hinting of the past, invite users to get out their own family photos and put them in a digital version. Soft, muted, sepia colors hint of the past in ways that make users feel like they were going down memory lane themselves.

Whereas Robin and Jonathon are more open about how they spin productions, Patricia Mavo has a specific lens that she imposes on her production. As an oral historian, Patricia uses her oral history heuristic as a motivating factor behind her web design.

## From concrete modes to abstract modes

While Robin, Jonathon, and Patricia's work highlights ways that producers work with more tangible and, perhaps, more familiar modes, producers also use abstract modes to create and advance their message. Case studies considered in the chapter so far cover many of the concrete modes in Table 5.1 used to spin a story. Yet, producers speak about the power of more abstract modes such as interactivity and hypertextuality.

To take an example from the case studies, Cassandra Mathers speaks at length about the strength of interactivity in "the expansive world" of *Club Penguin*. In *Club Penguin*, problem-solving and communicating with others are core practices that keep members coming back. Such interactive and interpersonal mechanisms allow members to move across parts of *Club Penguin* to do different kinds of things with different sorts of people and this is what users like and learn from. Cassandra's descriptions of modal choice in *Club Penguin*, from the use of newspapers as an architecture of participation, to the blog which allows users to engage with each other, to games applications which invite problem-solving skills, all spotlight how producers use intertextuality to spin a text's story. Intertextuality allows users to move between and among features in the expansive world of *Club Penguin* and it reinforces the multiple texts within the website as a text. As media ecologies (Nardi and O'Day 2000), texts are nested within other texts and some producers build on the affordances of interactivity and intertextuality to send across a message.

Similarly, in *Kuma\War*, hypertextuality and moving between and among The History Channel website and the *Kuma\War* designer pages foster hybrid understandings and practices and, quite simply, improve game-play. In understanding the nature and history of a battle, problem-solving during game-play becomes easier, faster, and even more contextualized. Hypertext affords mobility across hybrid texts, such as from facts about battles to game designer notes, so that users can make the most informed decisions. Ken and David's choices regarding *Kuma\War* exemplify how hypertextuality, as links and connections to other texts within a text, can help producers appreciate connections across multi-genre texts and also points to reading path and a movement between and among texts online. Such mobility around digital ecologies affirms how different it is to read and problem-solve in digital media.

More concrete modes such as written words work seamlessly with more abstract modes such as interactivity to speak to target audiences, their habits, their ages, and their interests. Such nuances could only be garnered from individuals actively involved in thinking multimodally.

## Conclusion: operating from modal choice

As these cases studies indicate, Robin, Jonathon, Patricia, and even Rachel identify the right mode during production to transmit what they want or need to say. Where Robin uses modes as metaphors, Jonathon relies heavily on the substantive power of visuals, and Patricia exploits the expressive nature of photographs and muted colors. Clearly, each mode works within and acknowledges the power of production structures such as time constraints or audience viewing habits, yet the modes that they choose to spin a story rest on what they deem as the best way to tell the story that they want to tell.

Such nuanced, hidden epistemologies to production logic need to be exposed, critically framed, and, probably most crucially of all, interjected into literacy pedagogy. Teachers and students should think about why a producer chooses certain modes over others and how to replicate the decision process during multimodal composition. With the larger implication of literacy teacher education and pedagogy in mind, modes telling stories operate from a belief that we are most motivated and engaged when we control how we make meaning. Whether it is color or hyperlinks, the level of engagement, satisfaction, and learning that happens when we produce a text or read others' text productions is so much more advanced and beneficial when it is shaped around our tacit practices and aesthetic sensibilities, or seen another way, driven by what we do and what we like. What chapters 3, 4, and 5 offer is language and dispositions to get teachers closer to ways of teaching to students' tacit multimodal sensibilities.

# 6

# LEARNING IN TODAY'S
# AGE OF COMPOSITION

[Before doing this film project] all I knew about was writing and using still photos; I never had any experience with film. So I went on a short course and got a little bit of technical knowledge. Very quickly I realized that technical knowledge is completely different from thinking filmicly . . . [Initially] all I could think about was writing. That was my mode, and so what happened was in terms of thinking about communicating an argument was *I thought still by writing*, and I wrote just a short three page essay in which I tried to communicate the argument and how to use the film to do this. And then I moved onto Adobe Premier *and quickly realized that I wasn't going to be able to do it.*

(Rachel Hurdley, Documentarian, 2008; emphasis added)

For her work on the ESRC-funded Project with B. Dicks, *Watching, Listening, Reading, Clicking: Representing Qualitative Research in Different Media,* Rachel explored "how it's possible to communicate and argue using different media and how audiences interpret the argument according to the medium that's used" (2008). And yet, before she could assess her audience responses, she herself had to learn how to compose in and for today's media-rich environment. To develop composing choices native to such environments, Rachel needed to "think filmicly" if she wanted to reach her audiences. Recognizing her traditional print-based training could not be the basis for this literacy, Rachel needed to learn tacit and theoretically informed understandings of what composing means today. She needed to learn today's literacies of design. We argue the same can be said for educators.

According to Kathleen Blake Yancey, former President of the National Council of Teachers of English, we educators need to develop theoretically informed pedagogies that respond to today's "Age of Composition" when people are writing as never before. In this Age, people are pursuing their literacy and learning less through direct and formal instruction and more through "extra social co-apprenticeships" (2009: 5), fostered in large part by the communication possibilities enabled in digital environments. These co-apprenticeship models are much like what Margaret Mead describes as pre- and cofigurative ways to deal with radical societal changes, where, instead of traditional top-down teaching of long-established ways, "children and adults learn from their peers" (1970: 50). Similar to Mead who notes that, in times of significant change, hierarchical models of reproducing traditional lessons don't work, Yancey asserts that in today's Age of Composition, traditional methods of pedagogical approaches need to be rethought. In particular, Yancey argues that since "we have moved beyond a pyramid-like, sequential model of literacy development in which print literacy comes first and digital literacy comes second and networked literacy practices, if they come at all, come third and last" (2009: 6), educators need to operate out of pedagogies that recognize there are "multiple models of composing operating simultaneously, each informed by new publication practices, new materials, and new vocabulary" (7). In brief, traditional pedagogies alone won't do in today's digitally mediated, networked world.

As educators cultivate new pedagogies, ones acknowledging that becoming adept in emerging practices and unfamiliar skills requires new dispositions toward learning, we argue that schools have much to learn from the extra social co-apprenticeships Yancey cites, and perhaps especially from the people designing the spaces where these apprenticeships occur. In short, educators have much to learn from producers of digital media. Consequently, *Design Literacies* examines these co-apprenticeships, the producers shaping these educational satellites, and the logic producers embed in these sites of widespread social interaction.

While many educators are aware that global and technological shifts are radically altering what people need to know in order to fully engage in their civic, personal, and professional lives, pedagogical shifts have not kept pace. This gap has been documented by many outside of academe, with several government and business reports (Peter D. Hart Research Associates 2008; Ofcom 2008; US Department of Education 2006) correctly highlighting the consequences of educational practices not preparing students for current and future societal needs. These same reports, however, offer suggestions that we contest. Rather than, for example, more standardized testing at the college level, we seek alternative ways to spark responsive reform and spur innovative pedagogies, and we find some ideas for how to do this in the everyday experiences of digital media producers—current innovators who are engaging with the changing global and technological conditions and are invested in learning and teaching others to do the same. Our research into the practices of digital media producers, we believe, can help us highlight patterns or dispositions that we in the academy can learn from as we imagine ways to foster similar patterns or dispositions in our students and ourselves.

## Inhabiting design literacies

The dispositions of those producers we interviewed varied, a finding not surprising since these producers came from diverse domains (e.g. the academy, community, industry), six different countries, and multiple generations, ranging from those in their twenties to those in their sixties. Despite this diversity, our participants shared common dispositions when producing digital media to solve their local problems. *Design Literacies* focuses on four specific dispositions and four overlapping dispositions that intersect with these.

The eight dispositions prevalent in the situated, textured, even idiosyncratic practices of the innovative digital media producers we interviewed undergird what we believe will be core design literacies in the 21st century. We call these design literacies keying off part of the United Nations Educational, Scientific and Cultural Organization's (UNESCO) definition of literacy: "literacy involves a continuum of learning in enabling individuals to achieve their goals, to develop their knowledge and potential, and to participate fully in their community and wider society" (2004: 13). We situate these literacies within design practices that explicitly help people rework given resources to better meet their goals and those desired by their communities. These design literacies help people orient themselves along a learning continuum most appropriate for today's co- and prefigurative society.

### *Dispositions for 21st-century composition*

Each *Design Literacies* body chapter focuses on problem-solving dispositions that producers share. Across macro level issues (e.g. designing architectures of participation) and micro level issues (e.g. developing sophisticated modal choices), several dispositions emerged as particularly salient.

#### *Design*

The core disposition to which the others relate centers on design. Design encompasses a variety of practices (e.g. remix; convergence) that share the goal of using available resources in new ways to better meet the designers' needs within contemporary conditions. For example, many producers wrestled with how to use digital media to investigate, create, and distribute new information, artifacts, and practices, and found that redesigning existing artifacts and structures was the best way to solve their problems, whether these problems focused on getting the message out about autism activism (Amanda), persuading new users to try eMusic (Steve), or finding ways for communities to repurpose commercial goods, often for more community-directed actions (Jake).

Schools share design's problem-solving goals, and often ask students to do a project or write a research paper that draws on previous ideas as they develop their own, original argument. We want to extend the possibilities for redesigning information in the classroom. Arguing that design practices are valued academic work that require "extensive research, filtering, recombining, remixing, [and] the making of assemblages that solve problems" (Johnson-Eilola and Selber 2007: 400), we push for more than the typical citation of previous work. Instead,

104

we want significant remixes of previous work so that students construct new contexts and fruitful juxtapositions to such a degree that they are making new meaning. Building on previous scholarship (Cope and Kalantzis 2000; Jewitt and Kress 2003; Street 2009), we argue that learning emerges from innovative use of remixed designs that respond to but reframe established information.

Educators around the world are picking up this practice, on large and small scales. On a large scale, researchers involved in the Berkeley Archaeologists at Çatalhöyük (BACH) project are making available their "recent archaeological research and excavations at the 9,000-year-old settlement mound of Çatalhöyük, in central Turkey," because this team believes richer learning happens (in this case, of history, archaeology, anthropology, the humanities, ecology, biology, physical and chemical sciences, etc.) when people participate in the meaning making process. Since the BACH team seeks "to foster public engagement through direct experience with the process of data interpretation, creating different contexts and meanings through digital remediation," they do so via remix, where learners are encouraged to "reuse materials to create videos, websites, and other multimedia 'remixes' for noncommercial purposes" (Çatalhöyük Research Project n.d.). Remix need not have an international scope. Locally, individual teachers can use digital media environments to help students rework commonly available resources in order to resituate meaning, as when a student embeds a video in a blog or wiki in such a way that this message is re-purposed to support the student's argument. Models of this abound, especially in our students' worlds, such as a YouTube video where Carl Sagan and Stephen Hawking "sing" about the cosmos via remixed old documentaries, synthesized voices and music, and added digital transition features (melodysheep n.d.). This active meaning making by repurposing available resources is a disposition we encourage educators to develop in their students.

### Creativity

A second design-based disposition shared across our interviewees is the need to foster creativity and innovation. For the producers we studied, creativity was bound up with other practices: when *Edgar & Ellen* provide multiple ways to present a storyline, they lower the risk of being "wrong"; when *Reading Rainbow* uses television to encourage children to read without "nailing their feet to the floor," they foster alternative ways to connect reading with play; when Sarah Robbins teaches with *Second Life* in order to avoid getting "tuned out," she encourages innovative ways of acting and thinking, often in relation to connecting with others. Across these examples, producers in our research spent considerable time and attention on constructing digital media environments that evoke creativity both in the invention of the sites and in what these sites invite others to do. To foster this creativity, successful digital media environments elicit active participation, highlighting how essential such participation is to create architectures that support student learning.

Teachers know this, and understand that traditional "stand-and-deliver" models aren't working for today's students. As University of Texas media professor Craig Watkins argues, students today have "a much more active way of engaging their environment, a much more active way of gauging the information landscape" than students did even a decade ago. We agree with Watkins's conclusion that teachers need to re-direct the traditional "one-way flow of content" that marks so much of contemporary pedagogy into practices that better meet the needs of today's active learners (quoted in Beja 2009: A8). Consequently, *Design Literacies* calls on teachers to find ways to foster meaningful interaction with and among students, and argues this interaction can merge John Dewey's (1938) long-standing ideas about participatory, student-centered learning with the possibilities of Web 2.0 learning (e.g. peer-to-peer learning; easy and multiple ways to participate; informal mentorship).

For educators, we quickly note that these creative spaces did not culminate in multiple-choice exams. Rather, creativity for those we interviewed was central to ongoing processes where participants were motivated to solve pressing problems, such as when gamers in *Kuma\War* worked in groups of mixed abilities to complete their mission. Clearly, motives may vary between those voluntarily participating and those compelled to participate by legal statutes or teacher demands. And yet, many we studied (e.g. Sarah's *Second Life* teaching; Amanda's fulfilling course requirements) found it easy to inspire or be inspired by the possibilities digital, networked production offers even in their course requirements. Moreover, while the possibilities for digital media production will be locally determined (e.g. accounting for the influence of sponsors and the resources available), our producers make clear that creativity can be promoted via structured play with contemporary meaning-making tools within architectures of participation, which, as chapter 3 explores, are changing everyday literacy practices in ways we should attend to.

*Spin*

A third disposition centers on the concept of spin. Producers get, take, or find an idea and spin a story around it. Spin moves a concept to a text through a series of steps. For producers we studied, there was a pattern of researching the market; consulting production teams (i.e. sales, marketing, editorial, etc.); devising design/s; testing out designs on target markets; and launching the product or text. Cassandra Mathers talked about how *Club Penguin* spun out of a need to have safe interactive social networking sites for the five years and up market. MyPopStudio.com grew from an interest in adolescents as critical readers of media texts and teacher awareness of how to dissect and analyze new media texts. Of the three producers featured in the spin chapter some were driven by artistic vision, some by a felt niche in the market, and some were experimenting with a product. The inspiration for a spin can come from virtually anything, but it often entails collaborative meetings and building on each others' ideas.

Since spin is an action—a method of weaving a story around an idea through collaborative, creative, innovative experimentation with multiple modes to best meet the needs of an audience—teachers can help students learn the art of spin through several stages. To teach "spin" teachers need to give groups of students an idea for an assignment and resources as varied as digital or multimedial or paper and craft materials; what needs to be taught are ways of rhetorically spinning a given idea. Once an idea is spun into a design or potential designs, student groups need to designate roles and responsibilities with someone on design, someone on project management, someone on distributing meanings across a medium or media, someone on technical aspects of the project. For schools that are low-tech, students can use physical materials and artifacts from home to complete a design and product. For schools that are high-tech, students can work in digital environments to complete a design for the text/product. In both low- and high-tech contexts, teachers and students shift from shaping phrases and openings and closing paragraphs to discussing, analyzing, and critically framing how to use angles, spatial relations, or color to spin an idea. In this way, modes become ways of expressing an idea, and therefore modes play an important role in the composition process.

## *Multimodality*

A fourth disposition deals with the process of choosing modes to spin a text's message. Modes and multimodal composition involve the orchestration of a series of resources so as to tell the story a designer wants or needs to tell. Choosing the right mode is an attuned, naturalized practice producers pick up over time and with experience. Robin's dripping faucet, Megan's description of Olivia's walk, *Kuma\War*'s intertextual motifs of real and virtual battles being fought all use modes that speak across audiences for a desired effect or response. Design decisions made to transmit messages are contingent upon several influences from the contexts in which designs are made: such as a freelance documentarian with lots of freedom of modal choice, to a CNN news editor who works within company policies and agendas.

Calling students' attention to modes unravels ideological and conceptual layers in texts, in a manner similar to critically analyzing perspective in a written text.[1] Working across more varied sign systems in multimodal compositions allows students, and teachers for that matter, to develop a language and heuristic for thinking about design-based, often digital texts. Expanding understandings of television shows, webpages, video games, etc. opens up more fine-tuned analysis of a chosen sound, visual or combination of both. Producing and designing multimodal texts inducts users into design literacies by asking a series of questions such as: What catches your eye? How does the design achieve this? What is the perspective of the viewer? Addressing these questions helps users interrogate and design multimodal productions in ways that invite analytical skills that are relatively absent from the literacy classroom today.

## *Overlapping dispositions*

Beyond those that *Design Literacies* calls out specifically, there are several over-lapping dispositions. Below we discuss four such dispositions, illustrating how collaboration, interdisciplinarity, trial and error, and production warrant special attention.

### *Collaboration*

One overlapping disposition is collaboration. For many interviewees, collabora-tion is essential to their work. Twila Liggett was perhaps the most explicit about this. Recognizing she needed a range of expertise to move *Reading Rainbow* from an idea to a reality, Twila consciously assembled a "team" of educators, videog-raphers, and entertainers who together helped her enact her vision.

This sort of collaboration does not happen as often as it should in classrooms, whether in student-to-student or teacher-to-student contexts. For example, stu-dents may work in groups to brainstorm ideas, edit each other's work, even create supplementary materials, yet students' main work is generally accom-plished alone (perhaps in response to plagiarism concerns). Instead of privileg-ing the residual but pervasive single-authored model, we call on teachers to have students work in groups, thereby debunking the myth of a solitary genius creating an original work. The value of this collaborative work was evident to the teachers in Brian Street's (2009) small-scale study with University of Penn-sylvania students, who found that collaborative writing and group editing of academic writing strongly benefits the students as writers. Students in Street's course collaboratively edited a student paper to pitch it at the "right" register, access the "correct" discourse, and work within the conventions (and assump-tions about conventions) of the given discipline. Such teaching fosters collabora-tion, critical framing, and is explicit about a medium. Digital media production can model such collaboration by encouraging students to help one another develop particular practices (e.g. organizing/designing arguments; selecting appropriate evidence) as part of their interdependence on a team. For teach-ers, such collaboration may also help coordinate the teaching of students of various expertise levels, whether that expertise is technical-, rhetorical-, or content-based.

A second form of collaboration—that between the students and the teacher— calls teachers to relinquish more control in the classroom. As Sarah Robbins makes clear in her *Second Life* teaching, this is not an abdication of responsibil-ity. Rather, it is a re-arrangement of responsibility that asks students to be more active participants in their own education[2] and asks teachers to make sense of the interactions in newly designed spaces by overtly providing critical frame-works to help students understand the ethical, legal and critical considerations that, we believe, are central to future design literacies. As the producers we interviewed highlight, genuine collaboration on digital media production can tap both students' and teachers' strengths.

*Interdisciplinarity*

A second disposition that crosses those explicitly discussed in *Design Literacies* focuses on the valuing of interdisciplinary work, a disposition tightly linked to collaboration. For those we interviewed, gathering experts in diverse fields is common practice, as producers try to unravel the complications involved in everyday problem-solving. For example, Colleen Fahey always worked with interdisciplinary groups, whether collaborating with children's promotions coordinators, brand marketers, franchise liaisons, and liability specialists, while developing McDonald's Happy Meals or, via her publishers, working with librarians, marketing directors, and children's advisory board members to develop *Edgar & Ellen*'s story lines.

In general, universities have been slower to embrace this interdisciplinary expectation, preferring to stay in what interviewee and Harvard educator Rebecca Haines calls disciplinary "silos." This was the case for Bob Camp, a producer not profiled as a specific case study in *Design Literacies*. In order to develop a new gaming degree at a community college, Bob sought out English scholars who specialize in narratives of epic quests (e.g. *Beowulf*, *The Odyssey*); computer specialists who work on code; graphic designers who focus on interface; and economists who teach systems theory. And yet, faculty members at this community college were primarily beholden to departmental structures (e.g. course rotations; survey coverage) that meant that although appropriate faculty members were present, they were not available for Bob's interdisciplinary project.

Extensive research supports the pervasiveness of dilemmas such as Bob's and highlights the difficulty of breaking higher education's long-standing patterns that value discrete, disciplinary, non-cross-over specializations. According to "Canon of College Majors Persists Amid Calls for Change," in the US, "the top 10 bachelor's-level fields of study in 2006–7 were the same as those of 1980–81" (Glenn and Fisher 2009: A1), suggesting a commitment, even in socially, economically, and technologically changing times, for students to gain established, disciplinary knowledge about a topic that is not easily grasped when surveying many disciplines. And yet, why not develop structures that complement this commitment to disciplinary work with integrated, less isolated views that can more fully show a topic's complexity and possibility? This sort of interdisciplinary work, happening "at the interstices of disciplines," argues former US labor secretary and current University of California at Berkeley professor Robert Reich, is where "[m]ost of the interesting work today is done" (quoted in Glenn and Fisher 2009: A10). To facilitate such work, educators like Columbia University's Mark Taylor want programs of study—from individual courses to majors—to be centered more on addressing pressing problems (e.g. issues surrounding water) than on historical disciplinary traditions (Glenn and Fisher 2009).

Although such significant changes do not seem imminent—especially in the arts and humanities where people do not receive large external grants for complex projects that are more likely to require a team, such as in the sciences—there are several smaller instances of interdisciplinary activity going on in higher education that offer models for more interdisciplinary collaboration. For example, inter- and multi-disciplinary work has some footholds in cross-program research centers, university-wide programs (e.g. gender studies, ethnic studies), and even consortiums across institutions of higher education (e.g. Consortium on Fostering Interdisciplinary Inquiry). For example, the Joint Information Systems Committee, the Arts and Humanities Research Council (AHRC), and King's College London have joined forces to create interdisciplinary research projects in the arts and humanities that share a goal to "study and advance the use and understanding of digital tools and methods for research" (Arts-Humanities.net 2008) This community of scholars and researchers strives to build contacts and connections with other individuals doing interdisciplinary work across multiple educational sites.

Our interviewees and these research findings call educators to facilitate integrative work in their institutions and in their classrooms. Instead of having students on an assembly line—where students gather discrete information each hour, a practice that makes education efficient to distribute but disconnected from other courses, and, at times, from students' lives—we encourage teachers to break down disciplinary silos and to highlight the connections between and among the 8:00 English class, 9:00 history class, and 10:00 science class. Through such integrative work, teachers may be more likely to engage students in the multifaceted, interdisciplinary angles of genuine inquiry projects.

*Trial and error*

A more subtle, almost couched disposition articulated by participants in this study is the need for trial and error before finding the "right" design. Mistakes are inevitable in this trial and error production process. Documentarian Robin Benger sought out many evocative details before he found the dripping faucet. CNN editor Jonathon Graves decided to effect still images only after he failed to gather audio and video of the Minneapolis bridge collapse. Warren Beavis, a graphic designer we interviewed, found mistakes inevitable in his process of moving from "developing logos for the old print media" to developing logos for digital media (2007). Media scholar Carrie Davis went through eight iterations and multiple usability studies before she found a "satisfying" interface for her blog. These and other producers talk about frustrations, roadblocks, epiphanies, or aha moments when everything came together, emphasizing that experimentation requires risk, which often brings mistakes. These mistakes are not final failures but, rather, highly valued signs of growth that allow producers to test, improvise on, and refine ideas, modes, or practices before producers find the best way to communicate their message.

We educators need to encourage such a disposition, craving less a "right" answer and more a deep investment in experimenting with a range of possibilities while searching for the most effective way to do something. In the process, producers may discover happy accidents that change questions and therefore possible solutions. These happy accidents can be central to students' learning new ways to think about a topic, and even stumbling onto new topics neither teachers nor students anticipated. Producers' dispositions toward being open to this happy accident calls educators both to promote a tolerance for making mistakes and to provide structures (e.g. open-ended, knowledge-producing prompts; engaged feedback on multiple and varied drafts) that guide producers toward new understandings of their project.

## Production

The final pervasive and overlapping disposition we address is production, which is central to design-based literacies since it is through production that people learn how to enact the designs that they hope will better meet their goals. These goals can differ—for Jake Telluci, production of new widgets facilitates promise of community development while for Steve Kortrey production shapes consumer choice in top-down, market-driven ways that, in his case, will lead to a purchase on eMusic—but the process of production is essential in determining how designers' aspirations actually work, or need to be re-worked.

We see production particularly tied to design literacies through problem-solving/problem-seeking practices. Producers are problem-solvers who redesign conventional responses by re-seeing and re-spinning given materials; they are also problem-seekers who create new ways to approach information so that they, and others across their digitally mediated networks who build upon their approaches, come up with fresh responses. The processes of production manifest this problem-solver/problem-seeker disposition central to design literacies—a disposition that accounts for but moves beyond the typical schooling practices of restating or critiquing. As we note in the introduction, production calls people to understand something in a unique way. When people bring their ideas to fruition, they deal with various problems that challenge how things were supposed to go, which helps producers understand the complexity of both their ideas and the communication of these ideas.

Educators can develop this disposition in their own classrooms when they ask students to produce knowledge and not merely re-produce already established information; when they guide students to ask manageable questions about the world around them and when teachers then provide the structures to help students come up with answers. These open-ended inquiry projects are harder to assess, are messier to encourage, and call on students to take more control of their learning, but these are the activities that can lead students to adopt a producer disposition. And, as we argue throughout *Design Literacies*, developing this producer disposition is pivotal for students in today's Age of Composition.

## Teaching design literacies

To foster the dispositions that are central to the design literacies our interviewees highlighted as essential for learning in today's Age of Composition, we call on educators to head Mead's advice for those, like us, living in a time of radical social change: "we must create new models for adults who can teach their children not what to learn but how to learn" (1970: 72). As teachers orchestrate the environments and opportunities for student learning, they do so by providing both the readings and course materials (Mead's what) and the activities that shape and frame this content and material (Mead's how). In an age of rapidly expanding information, the demands on education require us to change content and, as Mead notes, the ways teachers shape and frame this content. Digital media producers are useful models for how teachers can redesign their pedagogies to better prepare students for today's prefigurative society. Digital media producers like Sarah Intellagirl Robbins have, in just a few years' time, shifted from designing learning spaces that sought to provide a lot of information (Web 1.0 or the transmission model of education) to designing spaces that seek to develop participation structures for users' genuine, active engagement. Sarah and other digital media producers we interviewed understand both Mead's what and how.

For educators to experiment with how they can enact Mead's what and how, we call on those designing literacy curriculum and pedagogy to cultivate the design literacies dispositions so that students are able to understand a greater range of choices and therefore are better able to be competent problem solvers for the 21st century. This is no easy task. Since educators are often so grounded in a word logic, our advocacy of design-based pedagogies asks teachers to step outside of familiar ways of teaching students. And yet, if we accept that we are in a prefigurative age, wherein we learn from our students, we cannot help but construct more responsive pedagogies. Studying the lives, stories, and practices of producers can offer some ways to do so.

In addition to articulating key dispositions that emerge from digital media producers' practices, we also believe educators can benefit from developing a language to describe design literacies. Such a language can focus our attention on practices and pedagogies valued in today's Age of Composition. And yet, after conducting many interviews and trolling through data, we have found great variety in the ways digital media producers discuss their design processes. The producers we interviewed draw on language from multiple domains, each with specialized vocabulary reflecting that domain's histories and sponsors. Without giving up on the ideal of having researchers and teaching organizations craft a shared language, we posit that these diverse constituencies make such an ideal elusive. Therefore, instead of seeking a language with shared words, we forward a language that describes dispositions. These dispositions function as a heuristic for educators to reference as they think about the philosophies undergirding their own teaching.

Not all lessons from our interviewees translate into classroom practice. Many producers we interviewed are tightly intertwined with the marketplace, and, while education is tightly tied to commercial networks and we have much to learn from the marketplace (e.g. responsiveness to need; problem-solving), education is not essentially a money-making proposition. Therefore, with the strong caution that many marketplace tenets come out of contexts and histories that may not reflect the civic, social justice mission central to education, we argue that educators can learn from and adapt the lessons digital media producers teach. In the process of incorporating the design-based dispositions of producers into our pedagogies, we define for ourselves our goals (e.g. preparing students for their present and future civic, personal and work life), our needs (e.g. intellectual and material support to investigate these dispositions and logics), and our assessments of success so that we can shape curricular standards for ways students make meaning in today's 21st-century contexts. These will be our design literacies.

# AFTERWORD

*James Paul Gee, Mary Lou Fulton Presidential Professor of*
*Literacy Studies, Arizona State University*

Humans are creatures of language. Our very ability to form cultures and socie-ties is due to language. And yet cultures and societies have always seen language as potentially dangerous to the very social order it helps create. Before liter-acy, societies almost always restricted who could speak publically and officially. Often it was priests, leaders, and elders who spoke and others who listened. In many societies it was, and still is today, fine for people to speak and listen where and when they want so long as what they talk about is "mundane." But they dare not speak or listen to treason or heresy as these are defined by the powers that be.

With the advent of literacy, new problems of control arose. Silent reading is more dangerous than speech, because it is harder to "overhear" and police the treason or heresy of the silent interpreter. Writing is the most dangerous form of language of all because it can spread so far and wide and its author can hide behind a fictitious identity.

Premodern societies often used violence to restrict language. Even modern societies, well into the 19th century—societies like England and the United States—debated whether poor people should be taught to read (certainly not write) for fear that reading would lead to interpretations that questioned reli-gion and the status quo. Eventually, however, modern societies learned that there was a lot less to fear from literacy than had been thought. Modern formal schooling served to teach the vast majority of people to accept as "received wisdom" what elites produced in writing and in the mainstream media. Let us call this the "schooling effect."

The schooling effect relies on instilling in people a particular theory of lan-guage. This theory says that when we speak or write we are "following rules." Furthermore, language represents—re-presents—reality by packaging into words "ideas" that reflect the world. These words can then be transmitted to others who unpack them to get at the ideas and, thus, in turn, the world as it is. Finally, the story goes, there are people who "know the rules" better than others and see the world more clearly than others, thanks to birth or educa-tion. These are the people who do—or should—produce writing. Reading what they write—or watching what they produce on mainstream media—is the role of most people in society. This theory of language is now so common and long running in our schooled societies that we take it almost entirely for granted as obvious—or did until quite recently (so-called "primitive societies" often viewed language not as transmission but as performance).

Today, modern popular culture and the uses it makes of digital media can teach even quite young people a truth about language that schools have long hidden. Take video games as an example. When you start to play video games you treat them rather like reading and writing. Some professional designer "wrote" the game and you read it. But then you start to fail and you begin to ask yourself how the "rules of the game"—the ones the designer "wrote"— can be used to your advantage to solve problems your way and allow you to win. You see that the game as a designed object and see, too, that you can and should "deconstruct" its design so that you can understand it and use it for your own goals and purposes.

Then you can go one step further. You put in a "cheat" (a piece of code that changes how the game works) and make the game operate the way you want it to. As you put in the cheat and play the game, you realize that you just designed a part of the game yourself. You begin to see yourself as a co-designer with the game's designer. But then you realize that even playing without the cheat was a form of co-design, since you were already using the game's rules for your purposes, making them work for you.

The final step is that game companies (as they often do today) give players the software by which the game was made and let the player "mod" the game, that is, modify it in small or very large ways. Enough modding and the game looks less like it was designed by the "elite" game designer and more like the "official" designer is just along for the ride as a "co-designer."

The "logic" of gaming leads gamers to see games as designed; to see design as an invitation for modification and redesign; and to see designing as really collaborative co-design. Game designers who stay in business have long caught on to all this. In this sense, Will Wright's *Spore* is indicative of the future of gaming. *Spore* was designed by Wright's team of professional designers, but is made in such a way that players can design the creatures and worlds they play in. The best of what they design is circulated to other players and eventually the creatures and worlds originally made by the game's designers play less and less of a role in the game and the creatures and worlds designed by the players themselves play the predominant role. The game is truly co-designed by the "official" designers and the players as a community. Indeed, the day will come when the "official" designers' creatures and worlds will have disappeared, replaced by better ones made by the players as they design for themselves and redesign what other players have made.

So this is one thing young people can learn from video games. They can learn a similar message from other digital media. But this IS and always has been the logic of human language, as well. It has taken games and other digital media for us to rediscover this deep human truth. Speakers and writers do not just "follow rules." They use the rules of grammar to design their own meanings for their own purposes. Just like gamers, they seek to figure out how the rules can be used for their own goals. Grammar sets but the parameters for this design work. And, as Bakhtin said, a great deal of what we as speakers and writers say is co-designed with other speakers and writers as we "mod" (modify) their previously uttered or written words.

Meaning making is a matter of design and collaborative co-design. All speakers and writers—not just elites—are productive, creative, co-designers of language. Furthermore—just as with games—the more we come to a conscious and explicit recognition of the "rules of the game" (grammar and ways with words, in this case), the more we can understand and intervene in our social, cultural, and political contexts as savvy designers.

As people today catch on that digital media and language are tools for design and co-design, they have broken a good deal of the traditional policing of language, of who can speak, write, create, and produce and who cannot. As production proliferates through ever more complex and global networks and communities, it is harder and harder to restrict and police. The elites are left to whine that what "everyday" people produce isn't "professional" even as what "everyday" people produce often replaces what professionals produce (as in *Spore*).

But there is a problem. The realization that both language and digital media are tools for design and co-design of particular perspectives and purposes means that meaning making is always about "spin." It is always about a perspective on the world, not a transparent window onto the world and truth. Just as game engines are for building worlds of certain types, not one universal world, we design different views of the world through language, not a universal transcendent neutral a-cultural viewpoint. So, then, it is easy to lapse into a sort of postmodern relativism that, in fact, detracts from our sense of agency as designers: we can begin to think that everything is just one perspective among many relative to the designer's values and beliefs. Any perspective is as good as any other, we will say. We will ask: Who is to judge other cultures and communities?

But, reality bites back and real people get really hurt when some perspectives are enacted and not others. Not all video games are as good as each other. So, too, with perspectives. We have to make choices and we have to make the criteria of our choices clear. A view of meaning making (whether with digital media or language) as collaborative co-design requires, in the end, thoughtful debates about what is "right" and "true" in the sense of what makes for a better, more humane, more sustainable world. We want to make good games and good worlds. So Mary Sheridan and Jennifer Rowsell's *Design Literacies: Learning and Innovation in the Digital Age* has given us exciting insights about new media in the modern world while also allowing us to rediscover a very old truth about language.

# NOTES

## 1 THE PROBLEM-SOLVING LOGIC OF DIGITAL MEDIA PRODUCTION

1  As we'll detail later in the chapter, we use pseudonyms for our participants, except when they specifically asked that we use their real name and company, generally as a form of publicity and therefore reciprocity for their work with us.

2  Educators are increasingly attending to ways in which they can better prepare students for a changing world. For example, international bodies (e.g. the International Technology Education Association), individual countries (e.g. the UK, which has developed international technology standards) and disciplinary organizations (e.g. the National Academy of Engineering; American Association for the Advancement of Science) call for better preparation of students for the 21st century. These important steps, however, are not having a quick enough impact on everyday teaching, as we discuss throughout this chapter.

3  For some of the reasons Lev Manovich argues for "new media," we argue for "digital media." For Manovich (2002), "new media" means "the shift of all culture to computer-mediated forms of production, distribution, and communication" (19). Despite this encompassing idea of an important cultural shift, an idea we share, Manovich also believes this use of "new media" is different from the popular understanding framed by consumer experience. "Digital media" can also fall prey to this consumer framing but, as we argue, "digital media" seemed more readily understood by a general audience than did "new media," a familiarity that allowed us to more easily distinguish our definition of the term.

4  For consistency, we use the term "digital media" even though at least one of the producers used analogue.

5  Related to gaming and perhaps more acceptable to educators, the practice of universities using *Second Life* islands is pervasive. Among the extensive research on this practice is research on Schome Park, a second life community in *Teen Second Life* where people in the European Union are looking to develop alternative educational models for the 21st century. Led by Peter Twining of the Open University, this experiment has drawn in various stakeholders—students, parents educators, policy makers, etc. For one of many analyses of Schome Park, see Julia Gillen (2009).

6  One oft-cited example using digital media is a YouTube video, *Did You Know 2.0*. This video was originally created for a Colorado school to facilitate a discussion about contemporary education. Within a year, this video claimed to have started over 5 million conversations worldwide. Within two years, this video was watched 1,714,318 times (as of April 30, 2008). Clearly, digital educational documents such as *Did You Know 2.0* can distribute their messages in truly remarkable ways. In addition, this video details how, by the mid-2000s, technology digital media had

infiltrated the lives of youth: 21-year-olds have played 10,000 hours of video games, sent and received 250,000 emails or IM, and more than 50% of 21-year-olds have created content on the web; more than 70% of 4-year-olds have used a computer; the number of text messages sent and received exceeds the population of the planet; there are over 2.7 billion searches performed on Google/month; if MySpace visitors were real population, it would be the eighth largest country in 2006, and YouTube received far more (Fisher n.d.).

7 For an expanded view on this, see James Paul Gee's (2003) *What Video Games Have to Teach Us about Learning and Literacy*.

8 These studies focused on students' out-of-school literacy practices in part to make sense of chronic underachievement of some students, concluding that these undera-chieving students are not deficient, but rather that these students are often proficient in literate activities outside of the academic curriculum (Pahl and Rowsell 2006).

9 There are many historical studies of how people have used multiple modes (prima-rily visual) for years. See, for example, Carruthers (1992) analysis of the *Book of Kells*.

10 Some exceptions include research on how students, as professionals in business set-tings, make the transition to workplace writing (e.g. Beaufort 1999).

11 See Naomi Klein's (2002) compelling chapter that describes the difficult choices underfunded schools must make when trying to balance keeping schools function-ing without sufficient funding and becoming advertisements for businesses willing to sponsor education.

12 The many partnerships between businesses and applied academic areas such as engi-neering or business programs indicate this statement may apply more to people in the humanities.

## 3 "FEARLESS CREATIVITY"

1 Robbins' use of prosumer combines producer and consumer. Businesses have tapped prosumers as niche markets that can shape business practices. Media specialists have focused on how prosumers (e.g. fanfiction authors) can shape storylines of beloved media. Educators, slower to use this term generally because of the overt commercial overtones, may use prosumer to reflect how students are shaping their own educa-tion. In each setting, prosumer implies collaborative, open, and peer-driven ("flat") ways of making meaning instead of the typical top-driven source of information in previous iterations of business, marketing, and educational models.

2 See Fleckenstein et al. (2009) for a more recent take on the ecologies metaphor within writing research.

3 Two years after this interview, and after the global economic crises hit new busi-nesses hard, Star Farm was being run and redefined by Ink Blot, and Colleen herself was working both there and on a new initiative where companies (e.g. Coke, Schick) give valued customers music as a reward (Fahey 2009), illustrating the sort of con-vergence culture Steve Kortrey discussed with eMusic in chapter 2.

4 Guy Merchant (2009) describes what may be required for teachers to incorporate digital literacies in the classroom. This change from what Gee (2000) describes as the old factory model of education calls teachers to reinvent themselves, in part by "build[ing] their confidence and to experiment[ing] with new approaches." These strategies, according to Merchant, require an acknowledgment of the significant time and work needed to rethink the relationships within the classroom that digital litera-cies brings about.

5 K-16 educators are not the only ones thinking about how to construct environments that call forth the changes we hope to develop. For example, Harvard educator Sarah Lawrence-Lightfoot examines "the connections that can be drawn between individual learning, community building, and cultural creativity" (Lawrence-Lightfoot

2009: 8) in the life stage she calls the Third Chapter, for people between 50 and 75 years old. Like us, Lawrence-Lightfoot focuses on the nexus of many structural interstices, in her case at "institutional innovation, shifts in cultural priorities, and educational reform."

## 6 LEARNING IN TODAY'S AGE OF COMPOSITION

1 For example, moving from monomodal thinking to multimodal thinking invites more expertise in art history and in graphic design (Arnheim 1996; Kress and Van Leeuwen 1996).

2 This shift may be initially uncomfortable for teachers; NCTE reports that "two-thirds of all teachers report feeling under-prepared to use technology in teaching, even if they use computers to plan lessons, access model lesson plans, and create activities" (NCTE 21st Century Literacies n.d.: 15), and, we believe, this number could increase as students continue to outpace teachers in both technical abilities and facility in digitally mediated spaces.

# REFERENCES

Alvermann, D. E. (ed.) (2002) *Adolescents and Literacies in a Digital World*. New York: Peter Lang.

—— (2006) Ned and Kevin: An Online Discussion that Challenges the "Not-Yet-Adult" Cultural Model. In K. Pahl and J. Rowsell (eds.), *Travel Notes From the New Literacy Studies*. Clevedon, UK: Multilingual Matters.

American Association for the Advancement of Science (AAAS) (1993) *Benchmarks for Science Literacy*. US: Oxford University Press.

Aristotle (2003) *The Nichomachean Ethics*. H. Tredennick (ed.), J. A. Thompson (transl.). New York: Penguin Classics.

Arnheim, R. (1996) Beauty as Suitability. *Journal of Aesthetics and Art Criticism* 54(3): 251–257.

Arts-Humanities.net (2008) Accessed September 23, 2009. www.arts-humanities.net/node/about

BBC (August 11, 2004) Video Games "Good for Children." *BBC News*. Accessed May 8, 2009. news.bbc.co.uk/2/hi/uk_news/scotland/3553352.stm

Baker, E. A. (2010) *The New Literacies: Multiple Perspectives on Research and Practice*. New York: The Guilford Press.

Banks, M. (1998) Visual Anthropology: Image, Object, and Interpretation. In J. Prosser, *Image-based Research*. London: Routledge Falmer.

Barton, D. and Hamilton, M. (1998) *Local Literacies*. London: Routledge.

Barton, D., Hamilton, M., and Ivanič, R. (1999) *Situated Literacies: Reading and Writing in Context*. London: Routledge.

Bazerman, C. (2002) *The Language of Edison's Light*. Cambridge, MA: MIT Press.

Bearne, E., Ellis, S., Graham, L., Hulme, P., Merchant, G., and Mills, C. (2004) *More than Words: Multimodal Texts in the Classroom*. UK: Qualifications and Curriculum Authority.

Beaufort, A. (1999) *Writing in the Real World: Making the Transition from School to Work*. New York: Teachers College Press.

Beavis, C. (in press) *Games within Games: Advertising, Youth Culture and Computer Games*. In J. Marsh, M. Robinson, and R. Willet (eds.), *Play, Creativity and Digital Cultures*. London: Routledge.

Beck, J. C. and Wade, M. (2004) *Got Game? How the Gamer Generation is Reshaping Business Forever*. Cambridge, MA: Harvard University School Press.

Beck, R. W. (2005) Access and Affiliation: The Literacy and Composition Practices of English Language Learners in an Online Fanfiction Community. *Journal of Adolescent and Adult Literacy* 49(2): 118–128.

Beja, M. (September 11, 2009) Linked in with S. Craig Watkins. *The Chronicle of Higher Education* A8.

Benger, R. (August 21, 2008) Personal interview.

## REFERENCES

—— (n.d.) Madiba: Life and Times of Nelson Mandela. www.cogentbenger.com/docs/mandela.php

Blau, A. (2005) The Future of Independent Media. *Deeper News* 10(1).

Bourdieu, P. (1980) *The Logic of Practice*. Stanford: Stanford University Press.

Brandt, D. (1995) Accumulating Literacy. *College English* 6: 647–649.

—— (1998) Sponsors of Literacy. *CCC* 49: 165–185.

—— (2001) *Literacy in American Lives*. Cambridge, UK: Cambridge University Press.

—— (2008) The Status of Writing, How Equipped Are Our Social, Cultural, and Political Institutions for Sustaining a Nation of Writers? Talk given on April 17, at the University of Wyoming, Laramie, WY.

Butler, J. (2006) *Gender Trouble: Feminism and the Subversion of Identity*. New York: Routledge.

Camp. B. (February 12, 2007) Personal interview.

Carrington, V. (2005) New Textual Landscapes, Information, New Childhood. In J. Marsh (ed.), *Popular Culture: Media and Digital Literacies in Early Childhood*. London: Sage.

Carrington, V. (2008) Digital Cultures, Play, Creativity: Trapped Underground. In J. Marsh, M. Robinson, and R. Willett (eds.), *Play, Creativity and Digital Cultures*. London: Routledge.

Carruthers, M. (1992) *The Book of Memory: A Study of Memory in Medieval Culture*. Cambridge, UK: Cambridge University Press.

Çatalhöyük Research Project (n.d.) "Remixing Çatalhöyük." Creative Commons. Accessed September 28, 2009. wiki.creativecommons.org/Case_Studies/Remixing_%C3%87atalh%C3%B6y%C3%BCk

Cazden, C. (1988) *Classroom Discourse: The Language of Teaching and Learning*. Portsmouth, NH: Heinemann.

Conference on College Composition and Communication (CCCC) (2004) Position Statement on Teaching, Learning, and Assessing Writing in Digital Environments. Accessed November 16, 2008. www.ncte.org/cccc/resources/positions/digitalenvironments

Cellan-Jones, R. (November 5, 2008) *Games "to Outsell" Music*, video. BBC News. Accessed May 8, 2009. news.bbc.co.uk/2/hi/technology/7709298.stm

Chandler-Olcott, K. and Mahar, D. (2003) Adolescents' Anime-inspired "Fanfictions": An Exploration of Multiliteracies. *Journal of Adolescent and Adult Literacy* 46: 556–566.

Chumby (n.d.) Accessed February 20, 2008. store.chumby.com/

Coiro, J., Knobel, M., Lankshear, C., and Leu, D. J. (eds.) (2008) *Handbook of Research on New Literacies*. Mahway, NJ: Erlbaum.

Cope, B. and Kalantzis, M. (2000) *Multiliteracies: Literacy Learning and the Design of Social Futures*. London: Routledge.

Creative Commons (n.d.) Spectrumofrights comic 1. Accessed July 7, 2008. wiki.creativecommons.org/Spectrumofrights_Comic1

—— (n.d.) Splash page. Accessed September 11, 2009. creativecommons.org/

Cushman, E. (1998) *The Struggle and the Tools: Oral and Literate Strategies in an Inner City Community*. Albany, NY: State University of New York.

Daley, E. (2003) Expanding the Concept of Literacy. *Educause Review* (March/April): 33–40.

Davies, J. and Merchant, G. (2008) *Web 2.0 for Schools: Learning and Social Participation*. New York: Peter Lang.

Davis, C. (June 4, 2008) Personal interview.

Dewey, J. (1938) *Education and Experience*: New York: Macmillan.

Dyson, A. H. (1993) *Social Worlds of Children Learning to Write in an Urban Primary School*. New York: Teachers College Press.

—— (1997) *Writing Superheroes: Contemporary Childhood, Popular Culture, and Classroom Literacy*. New York: Teachers College Press.

*Educause* (n. d.) Writing the Web. Accessed November 25, 2008. connect.educause.edu/wiki/Writing+the+Web+-+blog?time=1227635402

Fahey, C. (October 12, 2007) Personal interview.

—— (July 2009) Personal interview.

Farr, M., Lisya, S., and Song, J. (2009) *Ethnolinguistic Diversity and Literacy Education*. New York: Routledge.

Finnegan, R. (2002) *Communicating: The Multiple Modes of Human Interconnection*. London: Routledge.

Fisher, K., with assistance from S. McLeod *Did You Know 2.0*. Accessed October 1, 2008. www.youtube.com/watch?v=pMcfrLYDm2U

Fleckenstein, K., Spinuzzi, C., Rickly, R., and Papper, C. C. (2008). The Importance of Harmony: An Ecological Metaphor for Writing Research. *College Composition and Communication* 60: 388–419.

Gee, J. P. (1989) Literacy, Discourse, and Linguistics: An Introduction. *Journal of Education* 171(1): 5–25.

—— (1996) *Social Languages and Literacies: Ideology of Discourse* (2nd edition). London: Taylor and Francis.

—— (1999a) *An Introduction to Discourse Analysis*. London: Routledge.

—— (1999b) The Limits of Reframing: A Response to Professor Snow. *Journal of Literacy Research* 32: 121–130.

—— (2000) New People in New Worlds. In B. Cope and M. Kalantzis (eds.), *Multiliteracies: Literacy Learning and the Design of Social Futures* (43–68). South Yarra: Macmillan.

—— (2003) *What Video Games Have to Teach Us about Learning and Literacy*. New York: Palmgrave Macmillan.

Geertz, C (1996) Afterword. In S. Feld and K. H. Basso (eds.), *Sense of Place* (259–262). Santa Fe, NM: School of American Research Press.

Gillen, J. (2009) Literacy Practices in Schome Park: A Virtual Literacy Ethnography. *Journal of Research in Reading* 32(1): 57–74.

Gladwell, M. (2000) Designs for Working: Why your Bosses want to Transform your Office into Greenwich Village. *New Yorker* 76(38): 60–67.

Glenn, D. and Fisher, K. (2009) The Canon of College Majors Persists Amid Calls for Change. *The Chronicle of Higher Education* A1, A8, A10.

Goffman, E. (1981) *Forms of Talk*. Philadelphia: University of Philadelphia Press.

Gonzalez, N., Moll, L., and Amanti, C. (eds.) (2005) *Funds of Knowledge: Theorizing Practices in Households, Communities and Classrooms*. Rahway, NJ: Lawrence Erlbaum.

Grabill, J. (2007) *Writing Community Change: Designing Technologies for Citizen Action*. Cresskill, NJ: Hampton Press.

Gravings, J. (December 7, 2007) Telephone interview.

Guzzetti, B. (2009) Adolescents' Explorations with Do-It-Yourself Media: Authoring Identity in Out-of-School Settings. In M. Hagood, *New Literacy Practices: Designing Literacy Learning* (41–58). New York: Peter Lang.

Hagood, M. C. (2003). New Media and Online Literacies: No Age Left Behind [online version]. Supplement to Hagood, M. C., Leander, K. M., Luke, C., Mackey, M., and Nixon, H. (2003). Media and Online Literacy Studies (New Directions in Research). *Reading Research Quarterly* 38(3): 388–413. dx.doi.org/10.1598/RRQ.38.3.4

—— (ed.) (2009) *New Literacy Practices: Designing Literacy Learning*. New York: Peter Lang.

# REFERENCES

Halliday, M. (1985) *An Introduction to Functional Grammar* (2nd edition). London: Arnold Press.

Heath, S. B. (1983) *Ways with Words: Language, Life and Work in Communities and Classrooms.* Cambridge, UK: Cambridge University Press.

Heller, S. and Vienne, V. (2003) *Citizen Designer: Perspectives on Design Responsibility.* New York: Allworth Press.

Hilligoss, S. and Williams, S. (2007) Composing Meets Visual Communication: New Research Questions. In H. A. McKee and Danielle N. DeVoss (eds.), *Digital Writing Research: Technologies, Methodologies, and Ethical Issues.* Cresskill, NJ: Hampton Press.

Hurdley, R. (2006) Dismantling Mantelpieces: Narrating Identities and Materializing Culture in the Home. *Sociology* 40(4): 717–731.

—— (May 2008) Personal interview.

Hurdley, R. and Dicks, B. (2008) *Watching, Listening, Reading, Clicking: Representing Qualitative Research in Different Media.* Funded by Economic and Social Research Council.

Hymes, D. (ed.) (1996) *Ethnography, Linguistics, Narrative Inequality: Towards an Understanding of Voice.* London: Routledge.

Jenkins, H. (2006) *Convergence Culture: Where Old and New Media Collide.* New York: New York University Press.

Jenkins, H. (December 10, 2007) Authors@Google: Henry Jenkins. Accessed October 2, 2008. www.youtube.com/watch?v=FbU6BWHkDYw

Jenkins, H. with Clinton, K., Purushotma, R., Robison, A. J., and Weigel, M. (October 19, 2007) *Confronting the Challenges of Participatory Culture: Media Education for the 21st Century.* Chicago, IL: MacArthur Foundation.

Jewitt, C. (2006/2008) *Technology, Literacy, Learning: A Multimodality Approach.* London: Routledge.

Jewitt, C. and Kress, G. (eds.) (2003) *Multimodal Literacy.* London: Peter Lang.

Johnson-Eilola, J. and Selber, S. A. (2007) Plagiarism, Originality, Assemblage. *Computers and Composition: An International Journal* 24: 375–403.

Joint Information Systems Committee (n.d.) JISC homepage. Accessed September 27, 2009. www.jisc.ac.uk

Journet, D. (in press) Narrative Turns in Composition Research. In L. Nickoson-Massey and M. P. Sheridan-Rabideau (eds.), *New Directions in Writing Studies Research.* Carbondale: Southern Illinois Press.

Kalantzis, M. and Cope, B. (2005) *Learning by Design.* Victoria, AU: Common Ground Press.

Klein, N. (2002) The Branding of the Universities. In *No Logo* (87–105). New York: Picador.

Knievel, M. and Sheridan-Rabideau, M. P. (2009) Articulating "Responsivity" in Context: Re-making the MA in Composition and Rhetoric for the Electronic Age. *Computers and Composition: An International Journal* 26(1): 24–37.

Knobel, M. and Lankshear, C. (2007) *A New Literacies Sampler.* New York: Peter Lang.

—— (2008) Remix: The Art and Craft of Endless Hybridization. *Journal of Adolescent and Adult Literacy* 52(1): 22–33.

Kolko, B., Nakamura, L., and Rodman, G. (eds.) (2000) *Race in Cyberspace.* New York: Routledge.

Kortrey, S. (August 15, 2007) Personal interview.

Kress, G. (1997) *Before Writing: Rethinking the Paths to Literacy.* London: Routledge.

—— (2003) *Literacy in a New Media Age.* London: Routledge.

Kress, G., and van Leeuwen, T. (1996) *Reading Images. The Grammar of Visual Design.* London and New York: Routledge.

# REFERENCES

—— (2001) *Multimodal Discourse: The Modes and Media of Contemporary Communication.* London: Arnold.

Kress, G., Jewitt, C., Bourne, J., Franks, A., Hardcastle, J., Jones, K., and Reid, E. (2005). English in urban classrooms: Multimodal perspectives on teaching and learning. London: RoutledgeFalmer.

*Kuma\War* (n.d.) Images. Accessed March 26, 2009. www.kumawar.com/UdayQuasay-LastStand1/multimedia.video.1.php

—— (n.d.) Mission Page. Accessed October 17, 2008. www.kumawar.com/Mission.php

—— (n.d.) Multiplayer Introduction. Accessed October 17, 2008. www.kumawar.com/multiplayer.php

—— Splash page. Accessed October 17, 2008. www.kumawar.com

Lankshear, C. and Knobel, M. (2001) Do We have Your Attention? New Literacies, Digital Technologies and the Education of Adolescents. In D. Alvermann (ed.), *New Literacies and Digital Technologies: A Focus on Adolescent Learners.* New York: Peter Lang.

—— (2006) *New Literacies: Changing Knowledge in the Classroom* (2nd edition). Maidenhead and New York: Open University Press.

—— (eds.) (2008) *Digital Literacies: Concepts, Policies and Practices.* New York: Peter Lang.

Latour, B. (1987) *Science in Action: How to Follow Scientists and Engineers through Society.* Cambridge, MA: Harvard University Press.

Laughton, M. (May 21, 2008) Personal interview.

Lave, J. and Wenger, E. (1991) *Situated Learning: Legitimate Peripheral Participation.* Cambridge, UK: Cambridge University Press.

Lawrence-Lightfoot, S. (2009). *The Third Chapter: Passion, Risk, and Adventure in the 25 Years After 50.* New York: Farrar, Straus, and Giroux.

Lenhart, A., Arafeh, S., Smith, A., and Macgill, A. (April 24, 2008) Writing, Technology and Teens. Pew Internet and American Life Project. Accessed September 4, 2008. www.pewinternet.org/Reports/2008/Writing-Technology-and-Teens.aspx

Lenhart, A., Hitlan, P. and Madden, M. (2005) Teens and Technology. Pew Internet and American Life Project. Accessed July 10, 2006. www.pewinternet.org/Reports/2005/Teens-and-Technology.aspx?r=1

Lenhardt, A., Kahne, J., Middaugh, E., Macgill, A., Evans, C., and Vitak, J. (September 16, 2008) Teens, Video Games and Civics. Pew Internet and American Life Project. Accessed December 10, 2008. www.pewinternet.org/Reports/2008/Teens-Video-Games-and-Civics.asp.

Lenhardt, A. and Madden, M. (2005) *Teen Content Creators and Consumers.* Pew Internet and American Life Project. November 2, 2008. www.pewinternet.org/PPF/r/166/report_display.asp

Lewis, C. and Fabos, B. (2005) Instant Messaging, Literacies, and Social Identities. *Reading Research Quarterly* 40(4): 470–501.

Liggett, T. (2000) Executive summary for *Reading Rainbow.*

—— (2002) *The Continuing Relevance of Reading Rainbow in Promoting Literacy Development in Children.* www.shopgpn.com/WebData/Content/132/File/Continuing%20Relevence.pdf

—— (October 17, 2007) Personal interview.

Luke, A. and Woods, A. (2008) Policy and Adolescent Literacy. In I. Christenbury, R. Boomer, and P. Smagorinsky (eds.), *Handbook of Adolescent Literacy.* New York: Guilford Press.

Lunsford, K. (in press) Conducting Writing Research Internationally. In L. Nickoson-

Massey and M. P. Sheridan-Rabideau (eds.), *Pragmatics and Possibilities*. Carbondale, IL: Southern University Press.

Malone, K. (August 2007) Personal interview.

Manovich, L. (2002) *The Language of New Media*. Cambridge, MA: MIT Press.

Marsh, J. (2005) Children of the Digital Age. In J. Marsh (ed.), *Popular Culture, New Media and Digital Literacy in Early Childhood* (1–10). London and New York: Routledge.

Mathers, C. (October 2007) Personal interview.

Mavers, D. (2007) Multimodal Design in the Representational Landscape of the Classroom. Plenary given at the Designing the School of Tomorrow: Advanced Technologies in Education Symposium, 4th Educational Symposium, Ellinogermaniki Agogi, Athens, Greece (November 2007).

Mavo, P. (May 2007). Online interviews.

McLuhan, M. (1964) *Understanding Media: The Extensions of Man*. London: Routledge Publishing.

Mead, M. (1970) *Culture and Commitment*. Garden City, NY: Natural History Press.

Melodysheep (n.d.) Carl Sagan: "A Glorious Dawn" ft Stephen Hawking (Cosmos remixed by melodysheep). Accessed September 19, 2009. www.youtube.com/watch?v=O_2WOMwYCnw

Merchant, G. (2009) Literacy in Virtual Worlds. *Journal of Research in Reading* 32(1): 38–56.

Miller, C. C. (September 20, 2009) A Quick Path to Magazine Editor and Publisher. *The New York Times*, technology section, B7.

—— (September 20, 2009) Learning English, in Virtual World. *The New York Times*, technology section, B7.

—— (September 20, 2009) Web Addresses, Customized. *The New York Times*, technology section, B7.

—— (September 20, 2009) Hackers Latch On to Excitement Surrounding Latest Potter Film. *The New York Times*, technology section, B7.

Moje, E (2000) "To be Part of the Story": The Literacy Practices of Gangsta Adolescents. *Teachers College Record* 102(3): 651–690.

My ePets (n.d.) Splash page. Accessed December 5, 2008. www.myepets.com/

Nardi, B. A. and O'Day, V. L. (2000) *Information Ecologies: Using Technology with Heart*. Cambridge, MA: MIT Press.

National Council of Teachers of English (NCTE) (2005) Position Statement On Multimodal Literacies. Accessed September 16, 2009. www.ncte.org/positions/statements/multimodalliteracies

—— (2007) 21st-Century Literacies: A Policy Research Brief. Accessed September 16, 2009. www.ncte.org/library/NCTEFiles/Resources/PolicyResearch/21stCenturyResearchBrief.pdf

Nielson Foundation (n.d.) Website. www.nielsonmedia.com

New London Group (1996) A Pedagogy of Multiliteracies: Designing Social Futures. *Harvard Educational Review* 66(1): 60–92.

New London Group (2000) A Pedagogy of Multiliteracies: Designing Social Futures. In B. Cope and M. Kalantzis (eds.), *Multiliteracies: Literacy Learning and the Design of Social Futures* (9–37). London: Routledge.

Norris, S. (2004) *Analyzing Multimodal Interaction: A Methodological Framework*. London: Routledge.

Ofcom (2008) Communications Market Report. Accessed September 28, 2009. www.ofcom.org.uk/research/cm/cmr08/

125

Olds, J. and Schwartz, R. S. (2009) *The Lonely American: Drifting Apart in the Twenty-first Century*. Boston, MA: Beacon Press.

Omerod, F. and Ivanič, R. (2002) Materiality in Children's Meaning-making Practices. *Visual Communications* 1(1).

Pahl, K. and Rowsell, J. (2006) *Travel Notes from the New Literacy Studies: Instances of Practice*. Clevedon, UK: Multilingual Matters Limited.

—— (2010) *Artifactual Literacies: Every Object Tells a Story*. New York: Teachers College Press.

Pew Charitable Trust. (April 24, 2008) Teens Do Not Consider a Lot of Their Electronic Texts as Writing. Press release. Accessed June 1, 2008. www.pewtrusts.org/news_room_detail.aspx?id=38268

Peter D. Hart Research Associates (2008) *How Should Colleges Assess and Improve Student Learning: Employer's Views on the Accountability Challenge*. Washington, DC: Association of American Colleges and Universities.

Pink, D. (2006) *A Whole New Mind: Why Right-Brainers Will Rule the Future*. New York: Riverhead Trade Publishers.

Porter, J. E. (2007) Introduction. In H. A. McKee and D. N. DeVoss (eds.), *Digital Writing Research: Technologies, Methodologies, and Ethical Issues*. Cresskill, NJ: Hampton Press.

Prior, P. (1998) *Writing/Disciplinarity: A Sociohistoric Account of Literate Activity in the Academy*. Mahway, NJ: Erlbaum.

Prior, P., Solberg J., Berry, P., Bellowar, H., Chewning, B., Lunsford, K., Rohan, L., Roozen, K., Sheridan-Rabideau, M. P., Shipka, J., Van Ittersum, D., and Walker, J. (2007) Remediating the Canon: A Cultural-Historical Remapping of Rhetorical Activity, A Collaborative Webtext. Kairos: A Journal of Rhetoric, Technology, and Pedagogy 11(3). kairos.technorhetoric.net/11.3/topoi/prior-et-al/index.html

Putnam, R. D. (2000) *Bowling Alone: America's Declining Social Capital*. New York: Simon and Schuster.

Qarooni, N. (July 1, 2007) Local CD for autism. *Star Ledger*, New Jersey.

Rhodes, J., and Robnolt, V. (2009) Digital literacies in the classroom. In L. Christenbury, R. Bomer, and P. Smagorinsky (eds.), Handbook of Adolescent Literacy Research (153–169). New York: Guilford Publications.

Rich, M. (2008a) The Future of Reading: Using Video Games as Bait to Hook Readers. *The New York Times*, October 5, 2008. Accessed October 8, 2008. www.nytimes.com/2008/10/06/books/06games.html?_r=1&scp=1&sq=using%20video%20games%20as%20bait%20to%20hook%20readers&st=cse

—— (2008b) The Future of Reading: Literacy Debate: Online, R U Really Reading? *The New York Times* 5 July 27, 2008. Accessed August 5, 2008. www.nytimes.com/2008/07/27/books/27reading.html

Robbins, S. (n.d.) "Intellagirl." Web 2.0 for Business: Revealing the Best Kept Secrets. Accessed October 20, 2008. www.slideshare.net/intellagirl/web-20-business-secrets

—— (n.d.) Splash page. Accessed October 21, 2008. www.intellagirl.com/

—— (n.d.) Talk for Mediasauce. Accessed October 20, 2008. (slide 3) www.slideshare.net/intellagirl/web-20-business-secrets/

—— (April 12, 2008) Personal interview.

Robbins, S. and Bell, M. (2008) *Second Life for Dummies*. New York: For Dummies publisher.

Roberts, D. F., Foehr, U. G., and Rideout, V. (2005) *Generation M: Media in the Lives of 8–18 Year Olds*. Kaiser Foundation. Accessed August 2007. www.kff.org/

Rosenblatt, L. (1995). *Literature as Exploration*. New York: The Modern Language Association.

Rowsell, J. (2000) Texts as Traces of Practices: Publishing Practices in Britain and Canada. Unpublished PhD, King's College London, University of London.

—— (2009) Artifactual English. In M. Hagood (ed.), *New Literacies: Learning from Youth in Out-of-school and In-school Contexts*. New York: Peter Lang.

St. George, D. (April 20, 2009) Study Finds Some Youths "Addicted" to Video Games. *The Washington Post*. Accessed May 8, 2009. www.washingtonpost.com/wp-dyn/content/article/2009/04/19/AR2009041902350.html

Scanlon, M. and Buckingham, D. (2004) Home Learning and the Educational Marketplace. *Oxford Review of Education* 30(2): 287–303.

Scribner, S. and Cole, M. (1981) Unpacking Literacy. In M. Farr (ed.), *The Nature, Development, and Teaching of Written Communication*. Hillsdale, NJ: Erlbaum.

Selfe, C. (1999) *Technology and Literacy in the 21st Century: The Importance of Paying Attention*. Carbondale: Southern Illinois University Press.

—— (2009) The Movement of Air, the Breath of Meaning: Audacity and Multimodal Composition. *College Composition and Communication* 60(4): 611–663.

Selfe, C. L. and Selfe, R. (1994) The Politics of the Interface: Power and its Exercise in Electronic Contact Zones. *College Composition and Communication* 11: 21–36.

Shaffer, D. W., Squire, K. R., Halverson, R., and Gee, J. P. (2005) Video Games and the Future of Learning. *The Phi Delta Kappan* 87(2): 104–111.

Sheridan, D., Street, B., and Bloome, D. (2000) *Writing Ourselves: Mass Observation and Literacy Practices*. Cresskill, NJ: Hampton Press.

Sheridan-Rabideau, M. P. (2008) *Girls, Feminism, and Grassroots Literacies: Activism in the GirlZone*. Albany: State University of New York.

Sloane, S. (1999) The Haunting Story of J: Genealogy as a Critical Category in Understanding how a Writer Composes. In G. E. Hawisher and C. L. Selfe (eds.), *Passions, Pedagogies, and 21st Century Technologies* (49–65). Logan, Utah: Utah State Press/NCTE.

Snow, C. E. (2000) On the Limits of Reframing: Rereading the National Academy of Sciences Report on Reading. *Journal of Literacy Research* 32: 113–20.

Snyder, I. (ed.) (2002) *Silicon Literacies: Communication, Innovation and Education in the Electronic Age*. London: Routledge.

—— (2008) *The Literacy Wars: Why Teaching Children to Read and Write is a Battleground in Australia*. St Leonards: Allen and Unwin.

Snyder, I. and Beavis, C. (eds.) (2004) *Doing Literacy Online: Teaching, Learning and Playing in an Electronic World*. Cresskill, NJ: Hampton Press.

Spellings Report (2006) A Test of Leadership: Charting the Future of US Higher Education. A Report Commission Appointed by Secretary of Education Margaret Spellings. Washington, DC: Education Publications of the US Government.

Spellmeyer, K. (2008) Review: A Massive Failure of Imagination. *College English* 70(6): 633–643.

Star Farm (n.d.) *About Star Farm* video. Accessed October 2, 2006. www.starfarmproductions.com/sfp-v2.html

—— (n.d.) Advisory Boards pages. Accessed October 8, 2008. www.starfarmproductions.com/sfp-v2.html

—— (n.d.) Press Room. Accessed September 30, 2008. www.starfarmproductions.com/sfp-v2.html

—— (n.d.) Properties Page. Accessed September 30, 2008. www.starfarmproductions.com/sfp-v2.html

Street, B. (1993) *Cross-Cultural Approaches to Literacy.* Cambridge, UK: Cambridge University Press.

—— (1995) *Social Literacies: Critical Approaches to Literacy Development, Ethnography, and Education.* Reading, MA: Addison Wesley Publishing Company.

—— (2009) "Hidden" Features of Academic Paper Writing. Working Papers in Educational Linguistics, University of Pennsylvania.

Strom, S. (November 13, 2006) What's Wrong with Profit? *The New York Times.* Accessed December 3, 2006. www.nytimes.com/2006/11/13/us/13strom.html?scp=1&sq=philanthropreneurs&st=cse

Takayoshi, P. (1994) Building New Networks from the Old: Women's Experiences with Electronic Communications. *Computers and Composition* 11: 21–36.

Takayoshi, P. and Haas, C. (2008) *What Is Writing Now? Writing on Mobile Devices and in Cyberspace.* Talk at Writing Research across Borders. Santa Barbara, CA.

Takayoshi, P. and Selfe, C. (2007) *Multimodal Composition.* Cresskill, NJ: Hampton Press.

Tapscott, D. and Williams, A. D. (2006) *Wikinomics: How Mass Collaboration Changes Everything.* New York: Penguin.

Taylor, P. (October 24, 2007) Personal interview.

Telluci, J. (2007) Personal interview.

UNESCO Education Sector (2004) The Plurality of Literacy and Its Implications for Policies and Programs: Position Paper. Paris: United National Educational, Scientific and Cultural Organization, citing an international expert meeting in June 2003 at UNESCO. Accessed October 25, 2009. unesdoc.unesco.org/images/0013/001362/136246e.pdf

US Department of Education (2006) *A Test of Leadership: Charting the Future of US Higher Education.* Washington, DC (pre-publication copy September 2006). Accessed November 3, 2006. www.ed.gov/about/bdscomm/list/hiedfuture/index.html

Van Leeuwen, T. (2008) New Forms of Writing, New Visual Competencies. *Visual Studies* 23(2): 130–135.

Warnick, B. (2002) *Critical Literacy in a Digital Era: Technology, Rhetoric, and Public Interest.* Mahwah, NJ: Erlbaum.

Wertsch, J. (2002) *Voices of Collective Remembering.* Cambridge, UK: Cambridge University Press.

Wysocki, A. F. (2008) Seeing the Screen: Research into Visual and Digital Writing Practices. In C. Bazerman (ed.), *Handbook of Research on Writing Research* (599–611). Mahwah, NJ: Lawrence Erlbaum Associates.

Wysocki, A. F. and Johnson-Eilola, J. (1999) Blinded by the Letter: Why Are We Using Literacy as a Metaphor for Everything Else? In G. E. Hawisher and C. L. Selfe (eds.), *Passion, Pedagogies and 21st Century Technologies* (349–368). Logan, UT: Utah State University Press and Urbana: NCTE.

Yancey, K. B. (2004) "Made Not Only in Words:" Composition in a New Key. *College Composition and Communication* 56(2): 297–328.

—— (October 31, 2008) *The Things They Carried: Research on Transfer and Its Implications for the Curriculum in Composition.* Talk at How Do College Students Develop and Transfer Writing Abilities? symposium, University of Denver.

—— (2009) A Call to Support 21st Century Writing. In *Writing in the 21st Century: A Report from the National Council of Teachers of English.* Urbana: NCTE, February: 1–9.

Zadroga, A. (May 14, 2007) Personal interview.

# INDEX

129